CONVAIR CLASS VF *CONVOY FIGHTER*

THE ORIGINAL PROPOSAL FOR THE XFY-1 POGO

Jared A. Zichek

RETROMECHANIX PRODUCTIONS

First published in the United States of America in 2017 by Jared A. Zichek, 12615 North Wildwood Point Road, Hauser, Idaho 83854, USA

E-mail: editor@retromechanix.com

©2017 Jared A. Zichek

All rights reserved. All featured text and images are copyright 2017 their respective copyright holders. No part of this publication may be reproduced, stored in a retrieval system, or transmitted in any form by any means electronic, mechanical or otherwise without the written permission of the publisher.

ISBN: 978-0-9968754-3-1

www.retromechanix.com

All images in this publication are scanned from documents held by National Archives II, College Park, MD, unless otherwise indicated. All color profile artwork is ©2017 Jared A. Zichek. Printed in USA.

Front Cover: At the top is a contemporary artist's impression of the Convair Class VF (Visual Fighter) Convoy Fighter proposal of 1950, which ultimately led to the XFY-1 Pogo. Below this is a speculative color profile of the original Convair design armed with rocket pods on the wing tips, each holding twenty-five 2.75" folding fin rockets. The overall Glossy Sea Blue scheme was typical of Navy aircraft of the early 1950s. (Note: this color profile is not to the same scale as those on the back cover).

1) Cover to the Convair Class VF Convoy Fighter proposal brochure dated 1 November 1950.

Introduction

The Convair Class VF proposal presented in this book is one of five proposals submitted by various companies to the US Navy Convoy Fighter competition of 1950. Unlike the Goodyear, Martin and Northrop proposals covered in previous volumes, Convair's submission was actually successful, resulting in the XFY-1 *Pogo*. While no great success, it was superior to its chief rival, the Lockheed XFV-1 *Salmon*, which will be covered in a forthcoming volume.

For those unfamiliar with the history of the concept, the idea of a turboprop tailsitter fighter emerged in the late 1940s, with the US Navy Bureau of Aeronautics (BuAer) beginning to seriously examine the feasibility of developing a vertical takeoff and landing (VTOL) tailsitter aircraft to protect convoys, task forces, and other vessels. These specialized interceptors would be placed on the decks of ships to provide a rapid defensive and reconnaissance capability until conventional carrier-based fighters could arrive and assist. The Battle of the Atlantic was fresh in the minds of Navy planners, who were concerned that the Soviets would engage in a similar campaign against merchant shipping if the nascent Cold War erupted into open conflict. BuAer's interest in a VTOL tailsitter fighter coincided with the development of new turboprop engines which provided enough horsepower to make the concept a reality.

BuAer's *Outline Specification for Class VF Airplane (Convoy Fighter) OS-122* was dated 10

July 1950. It listed the requirements for such an aircraft along with a scale demonstrator to verify the soundness of the concept. The document was distributed to the major aircraft manufacturers of the day, with the aforementioned companies responding in late November 1950. The products of this competition, the Convair XFY-1 Pogo and Lockheed XFV-1 Salmon, never made it beyond the prototype stage, as they proved to be very difficult to land, suffered from power plant reliability issues, and were eclipsed in performance by contemporary jet fighters. They became historical curiosities, regularly making the list of world's worst/strangest aircraft; the VTOL turboprop tailsitter concept proved to be a dead end.

Class VF Convoy Fighter Proposal

Design Analysis

In its proposal to BuAer, Convair noted that the design of a fighter aircraft capable of vertical takeoff and landing presented basically two new challenges. The first concerned the control of the airplane in vertical flight; based on BuAer model tests of this type of airplane and Convair wind tunnel tests of the proposed design, control in vertical flight was assured. A suitable autopilot was proposed for use in vertical and transition flying.

The second challenge was the two-position pilot's seat. The proposed seat was designed in accordance with BuAer fighter seat requirements and was positioned in the normal manner for the usual horizontal type of flight. For vertical takeoff and landing, the seat was rotated 45° forward in order to provide the pilot with the necessary downwards vision. Rudder controls followed the seat motion; however, the cockpit arrangement allowed the normal stick position to be used with both seat positions. The design of the cockpit provided for ejection from both seat positions.

The seat controls were designed to accomplish the following at the pilot's discretion:
1. The controls could be set so that a gradual transition of the seat from the vertical takeoff position to the horizontal flight position would take place as the airplane changed attitude from vertical to horizontal flight.
2. The controls could be set so that the seat transition would be completed by the time the airplane reached a 30° altitude.
3. The controls could be set in manual which allowed the pilot to place the seat in either position at any time desired.

Configuration. Preliminary studies by Convair showed that a delta wing configuration was superior in maneuverability and lighter in weight than a swept wing configuration when compared on an equal basis of meeting all of the performance requirements for the Convoy Fighter. The extensive work done by Convair on the XF-92A (7002) delta wing airplane including flight testing provided a reliable basis for the design as proposed.

Prototype

As requested in BuAer letter AER-AC-21 dated 21 July 1950, an unpressurized aerodynamic and dynamic scale prototype airplane (0.766 scale) using an Armstrong Siddeley Double Mamba III Turboprop was designed and included in the proposal. This prototype would be used to investigate vertical takeoff and landing and other flight characteristics as part of the development program for the tactical Convoy Fighter.

An alternative to construction of the scale prototype was to build an experimental full-size Convoy Fighter stripped of armament, electronic equipment, etc., but with the aerodynamic form maintained by mock-up armament. This experimental airplane would be powered by the existing Allison 5,525 equivalent shaft horsepower T-40 engine with single speed reduction gear, modified to operate through 90°. The proposed Convoy Fighter was powered by the advanced

---

2) Perspective interior arrangement of the Convair Convoy Fighter revealing how its compact fuselage was tightly packed with equipment.

3) Illustration of the pilot's seat, which could rotate 45° forward during vertical takeoffs and landings to provide the pilot additional downwards visibility.

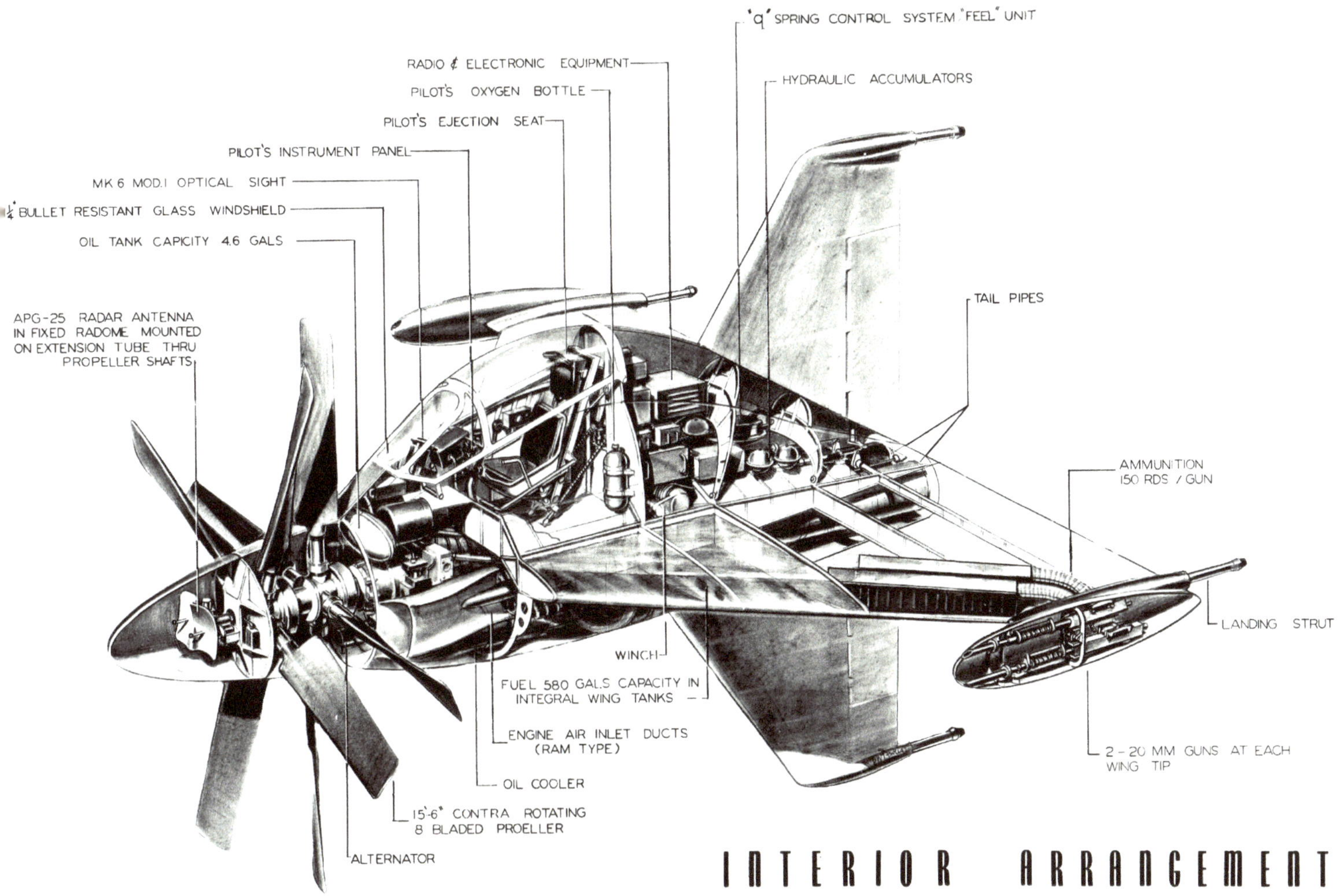

INTERIOR ARRANGEMENT

Labels (clockwise from upper left):
- RADIO & ELECTRONIC EQUIPMENT
- PILOT'S OXYGEN BOTTLE
- PILOT'S EJECTION SEAT
- PILOT'S INSTRUMENT PANEL
- MK 6 MOD.I OPTICAL SIGHT
- ¼" BULLET RESISTANT GLASS WINDSHIELD
- OIL TANK CAPACITY 4.6 GALS
- APG-25 RADAR ANTENNA IN FIXED RADOME MOUNTED ON EXTENSION TUBE THRU PROPELLER SHAFTS
- ALTERNATOR
- 15'-6" CONTRA ROTATING 8 BLADED PROELLER
- OIL COOLER
- ENGINE AIR INLET DUCTS (RAM TYPE)
- FUEL 580 GALS CAPACITY IN INTEGRAL WING TANKS
- WINCH
- 2 - 20 MM GUNS AT EACH WING TIP
- LANDING STRUT
- AMMUNITION 150 RDS / GUN
- TAIL PIPES
- HYDRAULIC ACCUMULATORS
- 'q' SPRING CONTROL SYSTEM "FEEL" UNIT

SEAT ADJUSTMENT FOR TAKE-OFF & LANDING

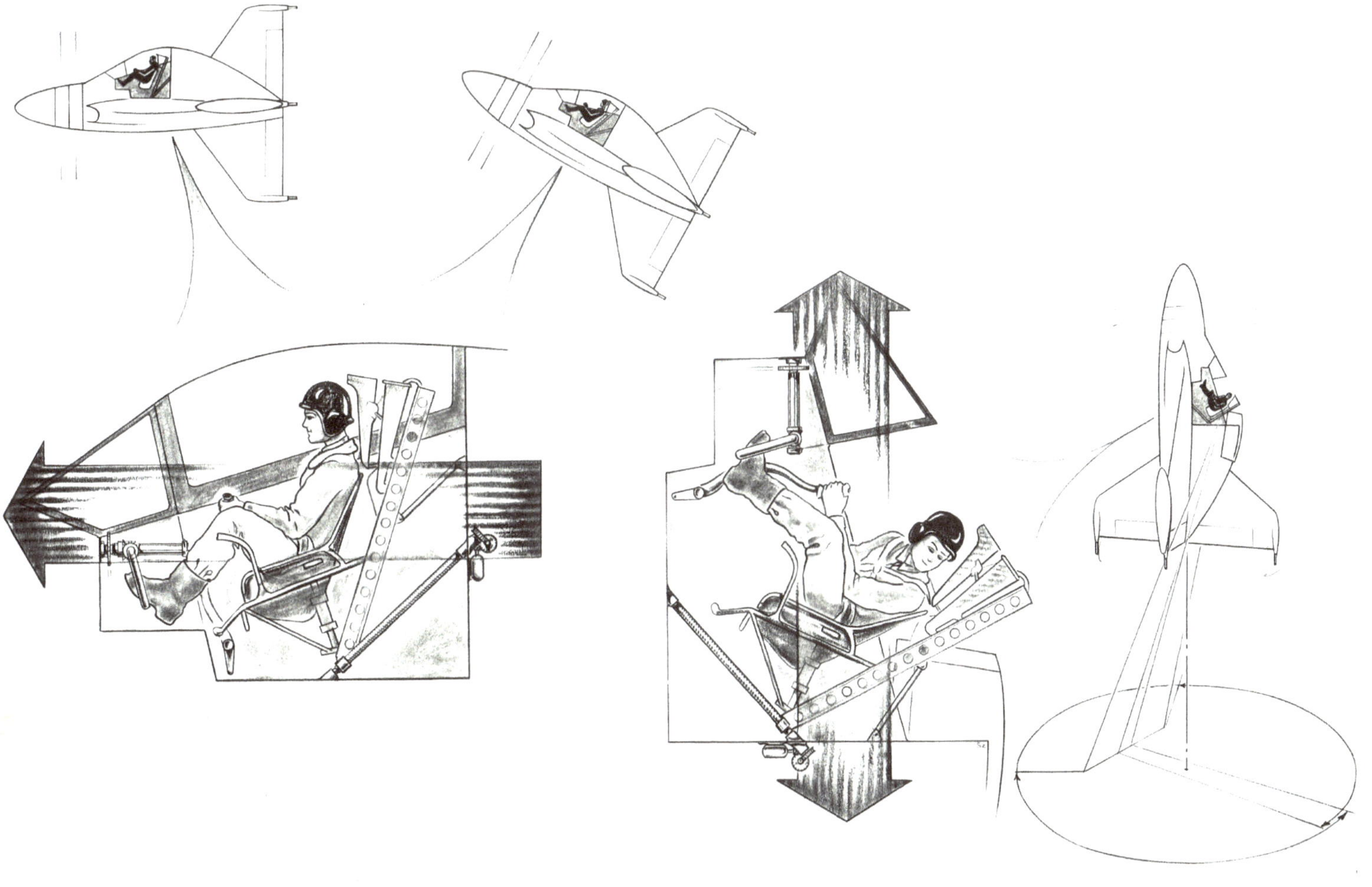

▲2 ▼3

TAKE-OFF

▲ 4

XT-40-A-8 engine having 7,500 equivalent shaft horsepower and two-speed propeller reduction gear.

This experimental Convoy Fighter had the advantage of being the same structurally and aerodynamically (except for power) as the tactical airplane and could be converted at a later date to a full tactical airplane by replacement of the power plant and installation of military equipment. It was pressurized, which allowed for testing at high altitude, thus simulating actual operation of the tactical airplane.

> 4) The Convair Convoy Fighter was designed for vertical unassisted takeoffs from a small platform on a convoy vessel.
>
> 5) When landing aboard ship in rough seas, the pilot could unreel a cable from the stern of the airplane and have the vehicle slowly winched downwards to achieve safe contact with the platform.
>
> 6) The Convoy Fighter could be refueled and rearmed with a minimum of support equipment aboard its home vessel.

General Description

Mission. The primary mission of this airplane was to protect convoy vessels from air attack by enemy aircraft. It was designed for vertical unassisted takeoff from, and landing on, small platform areas of convoy vessels.

The Convoy Fighter was also an effective tactical weapon for marine amphibious operations. It could be used for defense of an attack force en route to the objective area followed by support of the landing operations and establishment of the beachhead using LSTs as bases. Continued support would be provided, using mobile bases ashore, as the force moved inland. This use of Convoy Fighters would release CV and CVE carriers and their aircraft for other purposes.

Configuration. This airplane had a 55° delta wing and was powered by an Allison T40-A-8 turboprop engine with a two-speed propeller reduction gear.

The one-man crew was housed in a pressurized flight compartment equipped with an ejec-

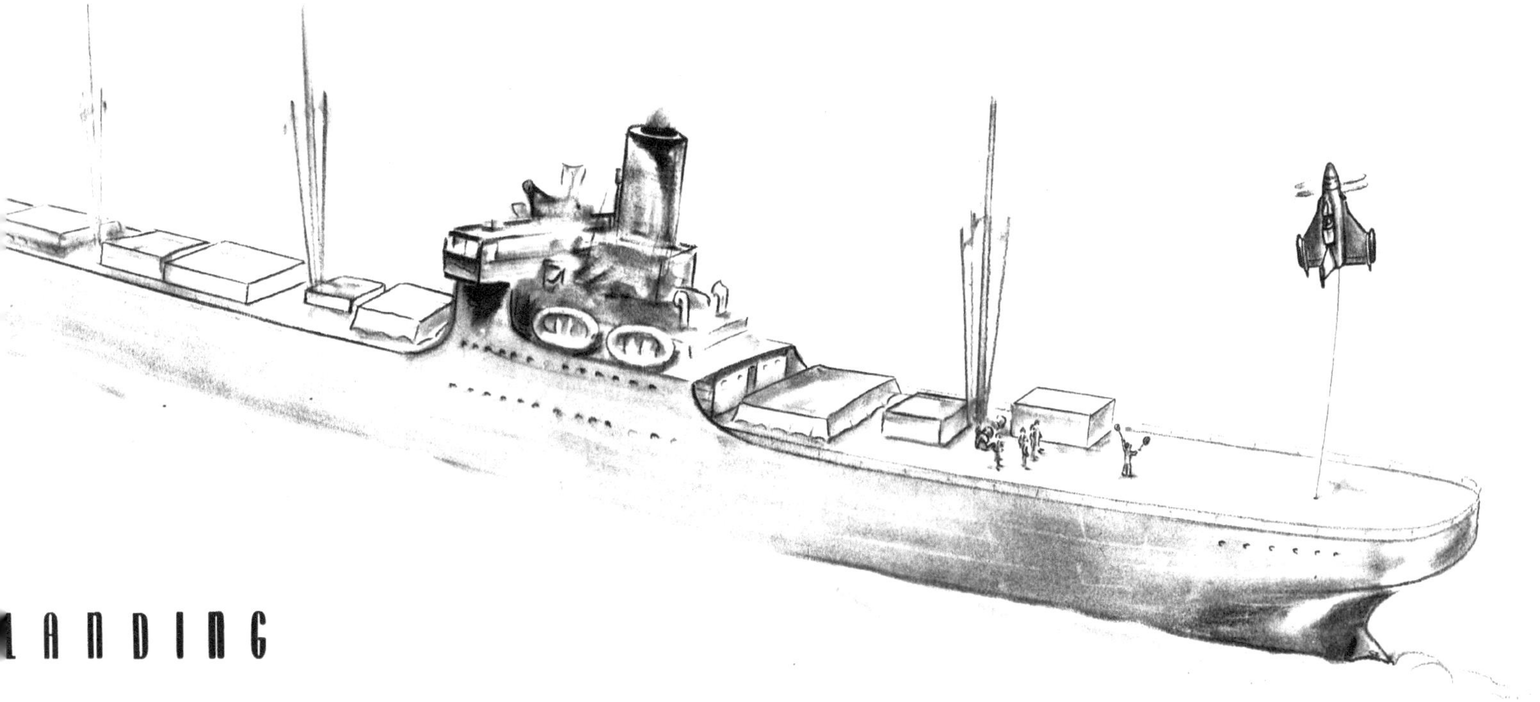

LANDING

▲5 ▼6

ARMING & REFUELING

OVERHAUL & REPAIR
▲7 ▼8

LST'S AT SEA

LSTs ACCOMPANY THE ATTACK FORCE TO THE OBJECTIVE AREA AND SERVE AS BASES FOR CONVOY FIGHTERS OPERATING IN SUPPORT WHILE THE BEACHHEAD IS BEING ESTABLISHED.

LST'S LANDING

AFTER ESTABLISHMENT OF THE BEACHHEAD LSTs MOVE IN AND UNLOAD VEHICLES AND SUPPLIES. CONVOY FIGHTERS OPERATE FROM THE BEACH IN SUPPORT OF THE LANDING FORCE MOVING INLAND.

AS THE LANDING FORCE ADVANCES CONVOY FIGHTER UNITS OPERATE FROM MOBILE BASES A FEW MILES BEHIND THE FRONT IN CONTINUING SUPPORT.

APU FOR GROUND STARTING AND HANDLING

INLAND OPERATIONS

▲ 9

tion seat built to Navy standards.

Four 20 mm fixed aircraft guns, with 150 rounds each, were installed in pairs at the wing tips. Good gun platform characteristics were achieved by the inherently high rigidity of the delta wing planform. Alternate armament installation allowed for the replacement of 20 mm guns with fifty 2.75" folding fin rockets.

All fuel was contained in two integral wing tanks.

Production Considerations. This design lent itself to high production assembly line methods of manufacture. Subassembly and feed-

> 7) A shipboard cargo winch being used in the overhaul and repair of the Convair Class VF Convoy Fighter.
>
> 8) The Convoy Fighter was also foreseen as a tactical weapon in support of marine amphibious operations using LSTs as bases.
>
> 9) As the marines moved inland, Convoy Fighters could use mobile bases ashore to provide continued tactical support.

er shop methods would have been used for mass production.

Landing

Landing aboard ship was accomplished from the hovering position by approaching the ship from the stern while drifting sideways with one wing pointed toward the ship. In this maneuver, the pilot had excellent visibility in the direction in which he was moving. If the sea was running such as to cause appreciable pitch or roll to the deck, the pilot, as he approached, unreeled a length of cable from the stern of the airplane which was caught by a man on deck, as was done when a blimp made contact. This cable was attached, by a quick connecting device on the end, to another cable that was unreeled from a winch below deck. This winch was operated by a fluid torque converter thereby eliminating any quick jerk and, at the same time, exerting a steady pull on the cable which assured a constant rate of descent of the airplane relative to the deck. As the airplane settled down towards the deck and

PERFORMANCE SUMMARY

PERFORMANCE DATA**

TAKE-OFF GROSS WEIGHT	LB	16,000
FUEL	LB	2,950
BASIC FLIGHT DESIGN GROSS WEIGHT (TAKE-OFF GROSS WEIGHT MINUS 40% FUEL)	LB	14,820
DESIGN LANDING GROSS WEIGHT (TAKE-OFF GROSS WEIGHT MINUS 60% FUEL)	LB	14,230
HIGH SPEED, BASIC FLIGHT DESIGN GROSS WEIGHT		
@ 35000 FT. ALTITUDE	KNOTS	542
@ SEA LEVEL	KNOTS	542
COMBAT RADIUS (BASIC MISSION WITH LOITER (1.53 HR)*, CRUISE OUT, COMBAT (3 MIN) AND CRUISE BACK AT 35000 FT)	N.MI.	100
AVERAGE CRUISING AIRSPEED		
OUT TO COMBAT AT MILITARY POWER (INCLUDING ACCELERATION PERIOD)	KNOTS	535
BACK FROM COMBAT ONE POWER UNIT INOPERATIVE	KNOTS	401
RATE OF CLIMB AT SEA LEVEL		
@ TAKE-OFF GROSS WEIGHT	FT/MIN	12,820
@ BASIC FLIGHT DESIGN GROSS WEIGHT	FT/MIN	14,100
TIME TO CLIMB TO 35000 FT ALTITUDE (FROM STANDING START)	MIN	4.48
RATE OF CLIMB AT 35000 FT ALTITUDE AT BASIC FLIGHT DESIGN GROSS WEIGHT	FT/MIN	5,100
COMBAT CEILING AT BASIC FLIGHT DESIGN GROSS WEIGHT (500 FT/MIN RC)	FT	46,000
FERRY RANGE (AT AVERAGE SPEED = 401 KNOTS) (16,530 LB. T.O. WT., 4480 LB. FUEL)	N.MI.	1492

*FUEL CAPACITY IS PROVIDED FOR 2 HOURS LOITER WITH A T.O. G.W. OF 16,455 LB.

** ALL PERFORMANCE AT MILITARY POWER UNLESS OTHERWISE NOTED

AIRCRAFT DIMENSIONAL DATA

WING		
TOTAL AREA	SQ.FT.	346
SPAN	FT. IN.	25'8"
ROOT CHORD	FT. IN.	22'8"
MEAN AERODYNAMIC CHORD	FT. IN.	15'7"
AIRFOIL SECTION	NACA	63-009(MOD.)
WING INCIDENCE AT ROOT	DEG.	0
AERODYNAMIC WASHOUT	DEG.	0
DIHEDRAL	DEG.	0
SWEEPBACK (LEADING EDGE)	DEG.	55
ASPECT RATIO		1.9
TAPER RATIO		5.23
VERTICAL FIN		
TOTAL AREA	SQ.FT.	150.6
SPAN	FT. IN.	19'4"
AIRFOIL SECTION	NACA	63-006.5,009(MOD.)
SWEEPBACK (LEADING EDGE)	DEG.	40
ASPECT RATIO		2.47
TAPER RATIO		3.15
FUSELAGE		
LENGTH	FT. IN.	29'5"
WIDTH (MAXIMUM)	FT. IN.	5'0"
DEPTH (MAXIMUM)	FT. IN.	8'10"

POWER PLANT

UNIT		ALLISON NAVY MODEL XT40-A-8 TURBO-PROP ENGINE
SPEC		ALLISON DIVISION OF GENERAL MOTORS CORPORATION SPEC #272-B REVISED 5-31-50
PROPELLER		8 BLADE DUAL ROTATING - 15.5 FT DIA., AF = 150 DESIGN C_P = 0.35 GEAR RATIOS = 13.65:1, 23.80:1

ENGINE STATIC SEA LEVEL RATINGS

CONDITION	RPM	PROP SHP	JET THRUST (LB)
TAKE-OFF	15700	6825	1685
MILITARY	14300	6955	1363
NORMAL (100%)	14000	5790	1225

▲ 10 ▼ 11

WEIGHT SUMMARY

WEIGHT EMPTY		11,785 LB
WING GROUP	1,574	
TAIL GROUP	426	
FUSELAGE	820	
ALIGHTING GEAR	300	
ENGINE	3,160	
ENGINE ACCESSORIES	290	
POWER PLANT CONTROLS	30	
PROPELLERS	2,105	
STARTING SYSTEM	30	
LUBRICATING SYSTEM	110	
FUEL SYSTEM	205	
INSTRUMENTS	50	
SURFACE CONTROLS	480	
HYDRAULIC SYSTEM	260	
ELECTRICAL SYSTEM	415	
ELECTRONICS	650	
ARMAMENT PROVISIONS	605	
FURNISHINGS	220	
AUXILIARY GEAR	55	
USEFUL LOAD		4,215 LB
PILOT	200	
FUEL	2,950	
OIL	80	
TRAPPED FUEL AND OIL	75	
GUNS (4) 20 MM	450	
AMMUNITION 600 ROUNDS	408	
EQUIPMENT	52	
GROSS WEIGHT		16,000 LB

approached within a few feet, the pull on the cable was increased to pull the airplane down and secure it, so that neither wind nor ship movement could cause upset. Analysis showed that even with a cable pull of 1,000 lbs, exerted at an

10) Performance summary and physical characteristics of the Convair Class VF Convoy Fighter proposal.

11) Convair's weight summary put their design at a gross weight of 16,000 lbs; BuAer's analysis put it higher at 16,724 lbs.

angle of 45° with respect to the thrust line, a rudder angle of 14.3° would balance the forces and moments in hovering flight.

Performance and Aerodynamic Characteristics

The basic concept of the Convoy Fighter gave rise to the following design requirements:
1. Extremely light weight.
2. Adequate stability and control at all angles of attack up to 90°.
3. Compact size and high structural rigidity.
4. Low drag at transonic speeds.
5. Freedom from buffeting at all speeds.

Extensive wind tunnel and flight experience with the XF-92A (7002) delta wing airplane led to early investigation of this type as an answer to the design requirements.

This experience demonstrated the following desirable characteristics:
1. Freedom from a sharply defined stall wherein lift and rolling control were suddenly lost at high angles of attack.
2. Low drag at transonic speed.
3. Freedom from buffeting.

In addition, the structural form of the configuration was ideal for light weight, rigidity and compactness.

Design studies and wind tunnel tests of a 1/10 scale model of the Convoy Fighter in the Convair 8 x 12 ft wind tunnel further confirmed this choice. It was shown that the airplane experienced uninterrupted and essentially constant positive stability in pitch up to 120° angle of attack, the maximum test angle. Directional stability to 120° angle of yaw was also retained. Positive control effectiveness in pitch and yaw was evidenced without the aid of slipstream velocity. With power on, the major part of the control surfaces remained in the slipstream and control

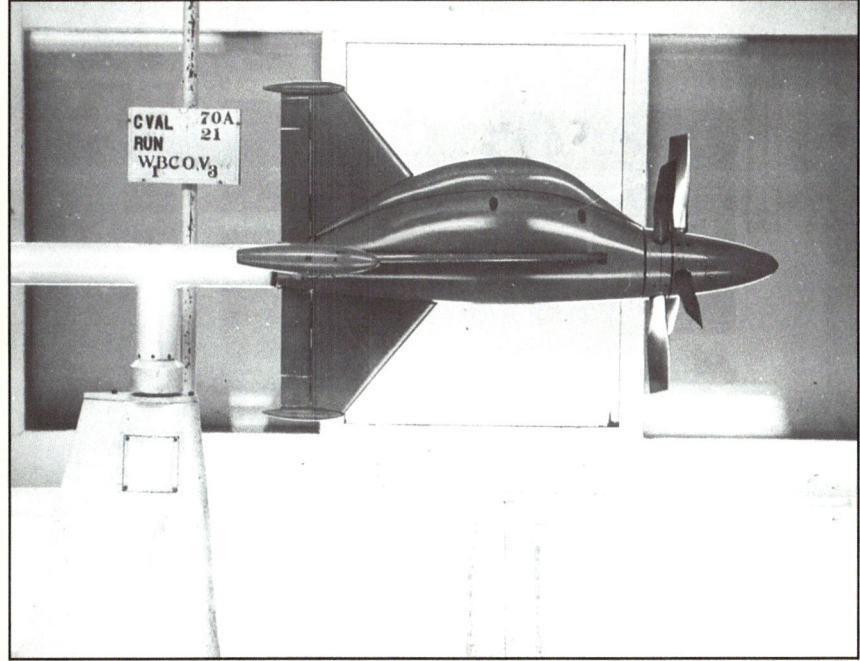
▲ 12

▲ 13

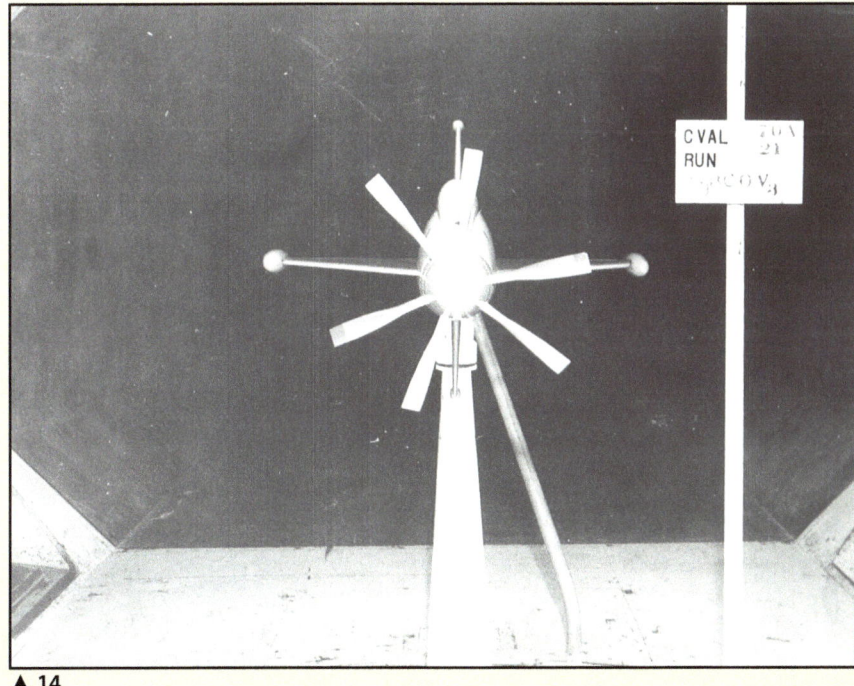
▲ 14

effectiveness was not impaired by extreme attitudes.

The rigidity and compactness of the delta planform configuration for the wing and vertical tail afforded the further advantage of allowing the airplane to be flown directly to its landing platform, rather than being captured and supported by an external structure. This rigidity and the accompanying small overall dimensions facilitated handling under adverse conditions.

A 9% thick NACA 63-009 wing section (with cusp removed) was selected on the basis of good high speed performance and adequate thickness for structural rigidity and space for fuel. A leading edge sweep of 55° was selected from considerations of stability and drag at high angles of attack, and low structural weight.

Longitudinal and lateral control were obtained by the use of short-chord, full-span elevons located at the trailing edge of the wing. Conventional rudder control was provided in both the upper and lower portions of the vertical tail. All controls were power operated. For the conditions of hovering flight, an autopilot maintained stability about any given angular attitude selected by the pilot.

Wind Tunnel Test

Tests of 1/10 scale powered model of the Convoy Fighter were made in the Convair 8 x 12 ft wind tunnel to obtain basic stability and control characteristics. The model was to scale except that no airflow

12-14) Photos of the original Convair Class VF Convoy Fighter model in the wind tunnel. Six blade propellers were substituted for eight blade units as they were more readily available.

through the ducts was simulated and six blade propellers were used instead of eight blade as these were readily available.

As previously indicated by extensive wind tunnel and flight tests of the XF-92A (7002) delta wing airplane, it was possible to develop a configuration, after a number of changes, having satisfactory stability and control about all axes up to 90° angle of attack, thus ensuring satisfactory transition between the vertical and horizontal flight attitudes.

Test data were obtained for the proposed design through angle of attack and angle of yaw ranges from 0° to 120°. Of particular interest was the fact that pitching moment and yawing movement curves were stable and uniform with no erratic breaks throughout the entire 120° range in pitch and yaw respectively.

Stress Analysis and Weights

The unique structural design of the Convoy Fighter provided ease of manufacture, low weight and efficient maintenance. In this design, the delta wing carried all the major loads such as power plant, pilot's compartment, equipment and fin reactions. The fuselage was therefore essentially non-structural, which permitted the extensive use of large, quickly openable doors and removable panels.

The delta planform of the wing and vertical surfaces was particularly suitable for installation of vertical takeoff and landing gear. Four oleo struts were mounted in faired pods at the tips of the surfaces. The inherent rigidity of the delta planform resulted in a minimum of added structural weight to take landing gear loads.

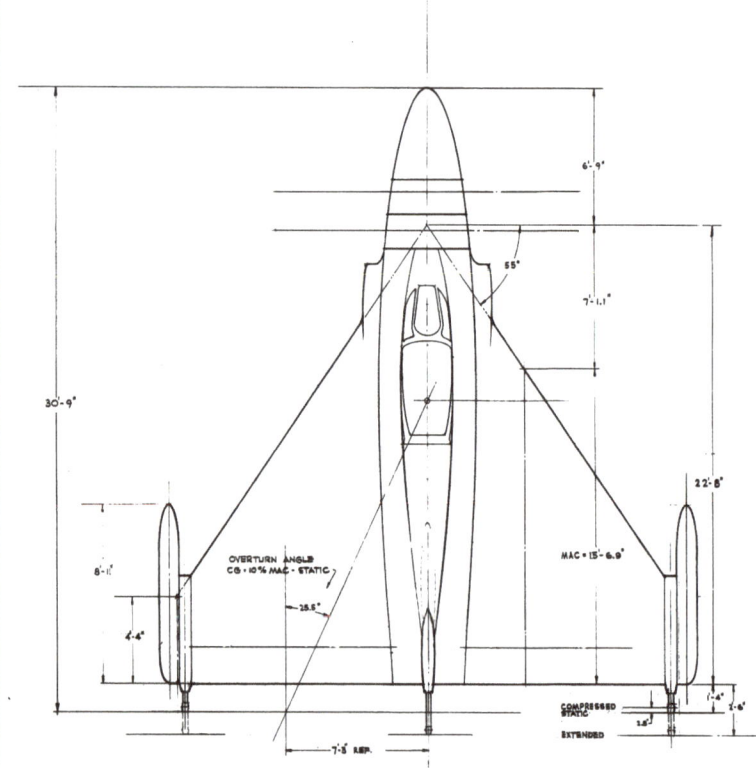

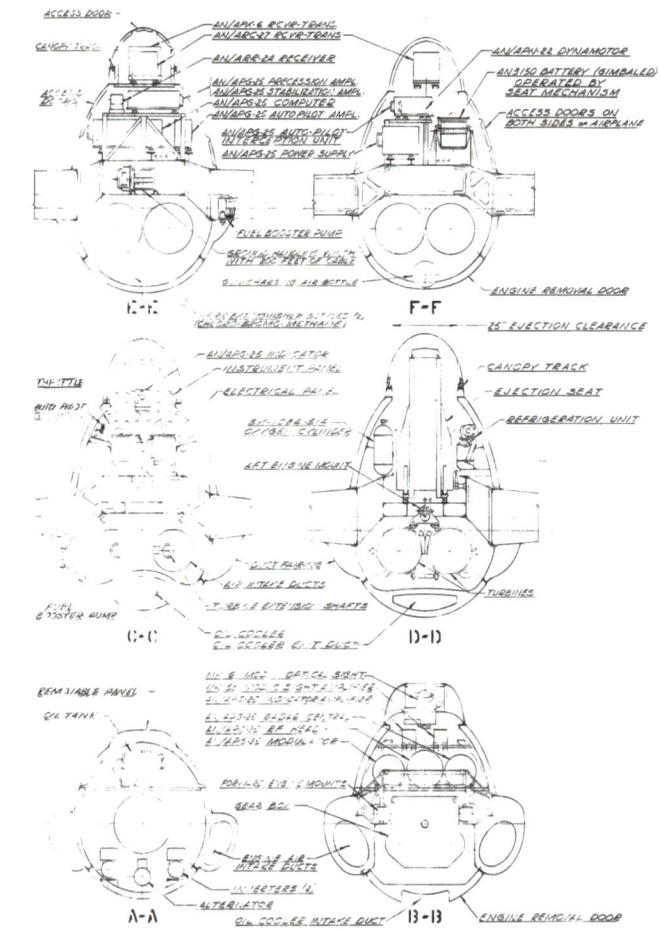

15) General arrangement drawing of the Convair Class VF Convoy Fighter.

16) Inboard profile and cross sections of Convair's VTOL tailsitter.

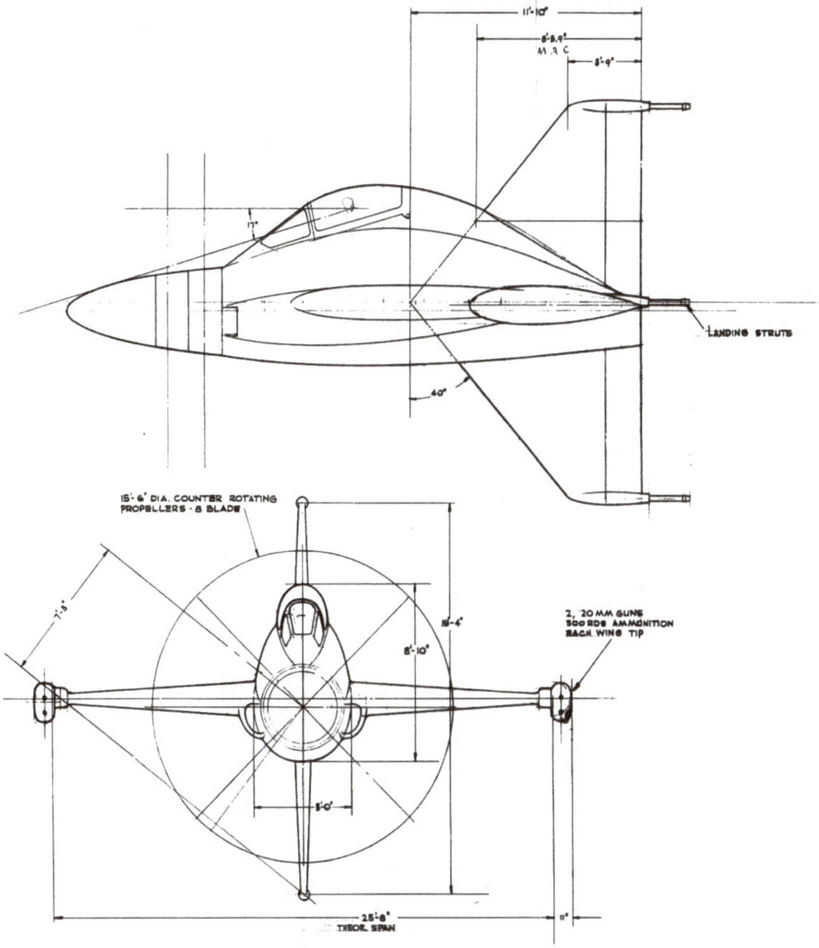

DATA

GROSS WEIGHT	LB	16000
WING LOADING	LB/SQ FT	46.2
POWER LOADING T.O.	LB/ESHP	2.13
WING-		
AREA (TOTAL TO ℄)	SQ FT	346
ASPECT RATIO		1.9
TAPER RATIO		3.28
SWEEPBACK - L.E.	DEGREES	36
AIRFOIL		NACA 63-009 MODIFIED
ELEVONS - AREA	SQ FT	28.2
DEFLECTION	DEGREES	±30
VERTICAL FINS-		
AREA (TOTAL TO ℄)	SQ FT	130.6
ASPECT RATIO		2.47
TAPER RATIO		3.15
SWEEPBACK - L.E.	DEGREES	40
AIRFOIL - ROOT		NACA 63-006.5 MOD.
TIP		" 63-009 "
RUDDERS - AREA	SQ FT	20.75
DEFLECTION	DEGREES	±30
POWER PLANT-		
MFR & DESIG.		ALLISON T40-A-6
TYPE		TURBO PROP
ESHP T.O.		7500

Convair
PRELIMINARY DESIGN DRAWING
GENERAL ARRANGEMENT
CLASS VF AIRPLANE - CONVOY FIGHTER
CONSOLIDATED VULTEE AIRCRAFT CORPORATION
SAN DIEGO, CALIFORNIA
SD-50-15001

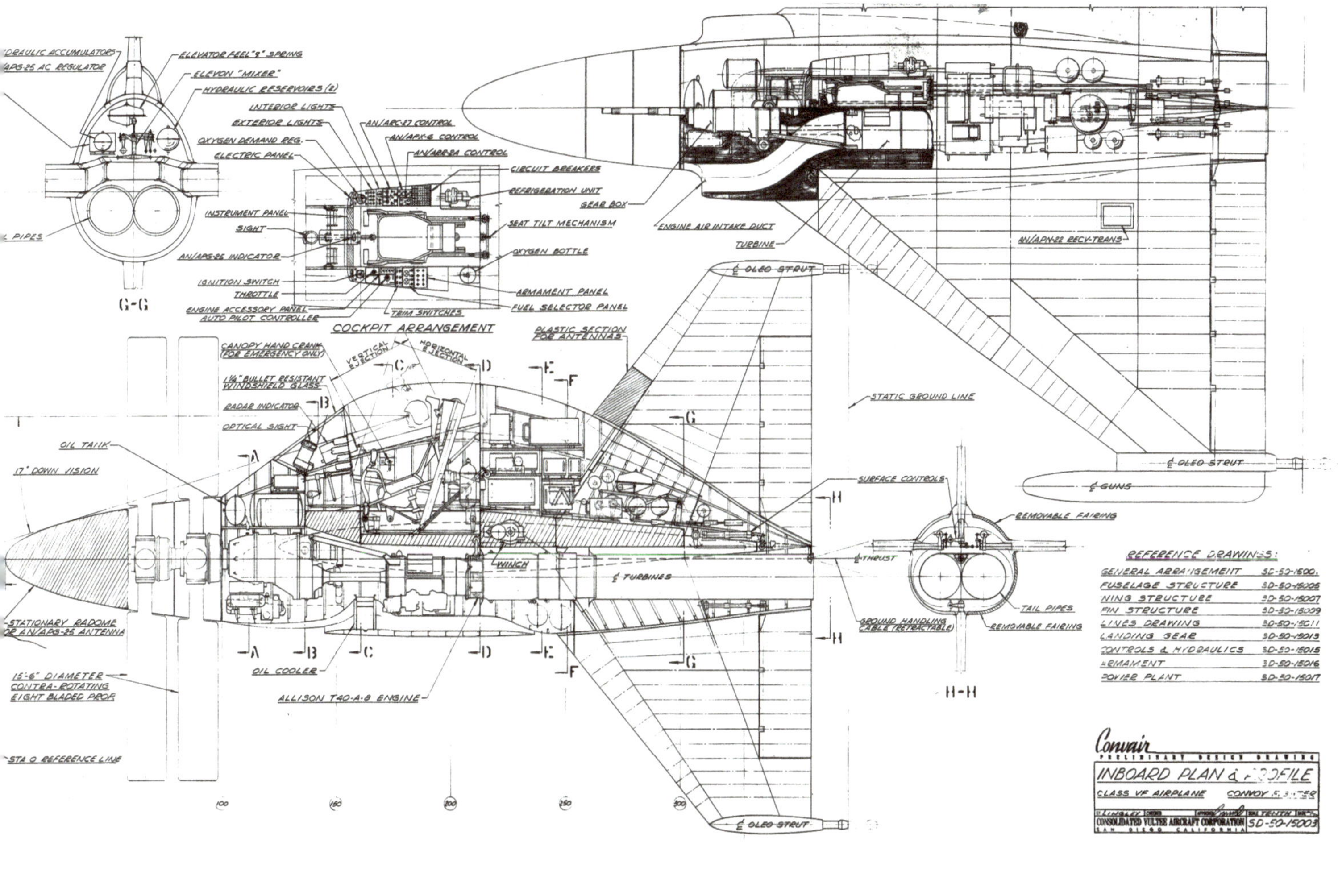

Convair
PRELIMINARY DESIGN DRAWING
INBOARD PLAN & PROFILE
CLASS VF AIRPLANE - CONVOY FIGHTER
CONSOLIDATED VULTEE AIRCRAFT CORPORATION
SAN DIEGO, CALIFORNIA
SD-50-15003

REFERENCE DRAWINGS:

GENERAL ARRANGEMENT	SD-50-15001
FUSELAGE STRUCTURE	SD-50-15006
WING STRUCTURE	SD-50-15007
FIN STRUCTURE	SD-50-15009
LINES DRAWING	SD-50-15011
LANDING GEAR	SD-50-15013
CONTROLS & HYDRAULICS	SD-50-15015
ARMAMENT	SD-50-15016
POWER PLANT	SD-50-15017

WING STATIONS (INCHES FROM ℄)
0
32
52.5
73
95
118
(THEO TIP)
154
℄ AIRPLANE
BODY STATIONS
℄ ELEVON HINGE
AN/APN-22 (REF)
RADIO ALTIMETER
READILY REMOVABLE STRUCTURAL DOORS FOR ACCESS TO AMMO. BOXES. (UPPER SURFACE)
INTEGRAL FUEL TANKS
580 GALS. CAPACITY PER AIRPLANE
SECTION A-A
BODY STRUCTURE (REF)
(SEE DWG. 5D-50-15005)
LANDING GEAR HOUSING. FOR INSTALLATION SEE DWG. 5D-50-15015
GUN INSTALLATION (REF)
(SEE DWG. 5D-50-15016)

▲ 17 ▼ 18

POWER PLANT ACCESS DOOR
WING LEADING EDGE FAIRING
WING-FUSELAGE DRAG ANGLE
AFT PRESSURE BULKHEAD
"WAFFLE" CONSTRUCTION ACCESS PANELS
FORWARD PRESSURE BULKHEAD
REMOVABLE COWL PANEL
℄ LATCH
℄ HINGE & LATCH
POWER PLANT ACCESS DOOR
℄ HINGE & LATCH
℄ LATCH
PORTION OF FUSELAGE BETWEEN FIN SPARS IS BUILT INTEGRAL WITH FIN
REMOVABLE FAIRING PANELS - AFT OF REAR FIN SPAR

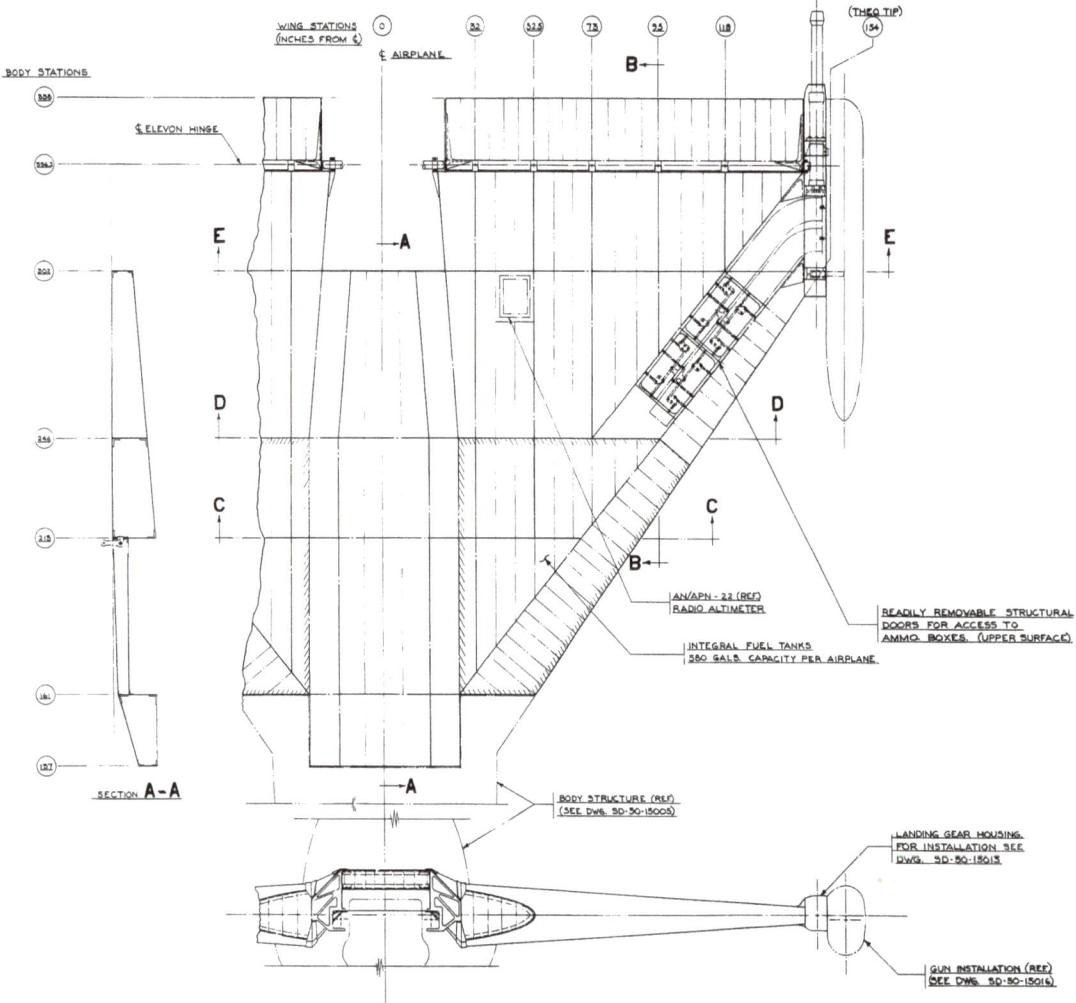

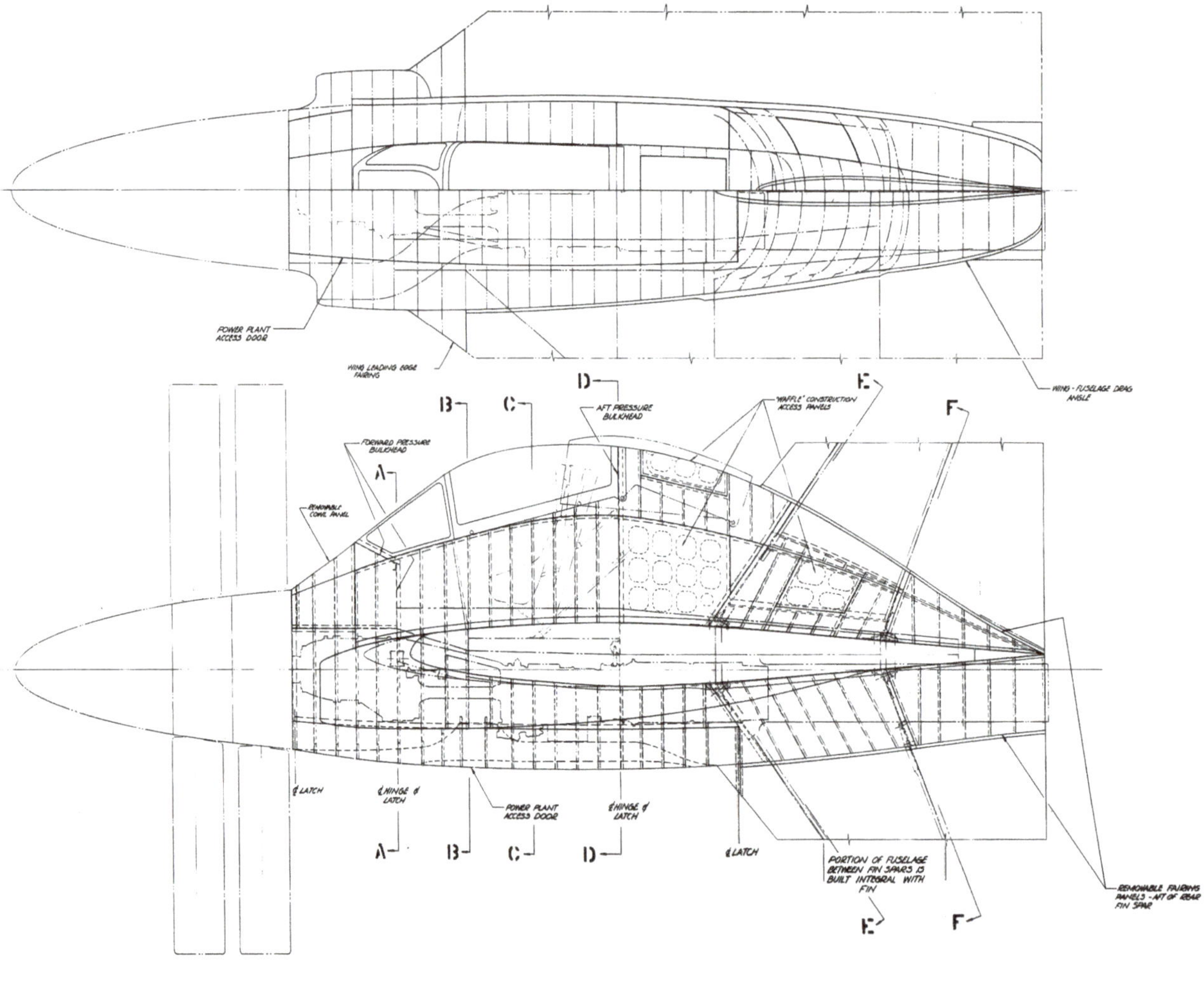

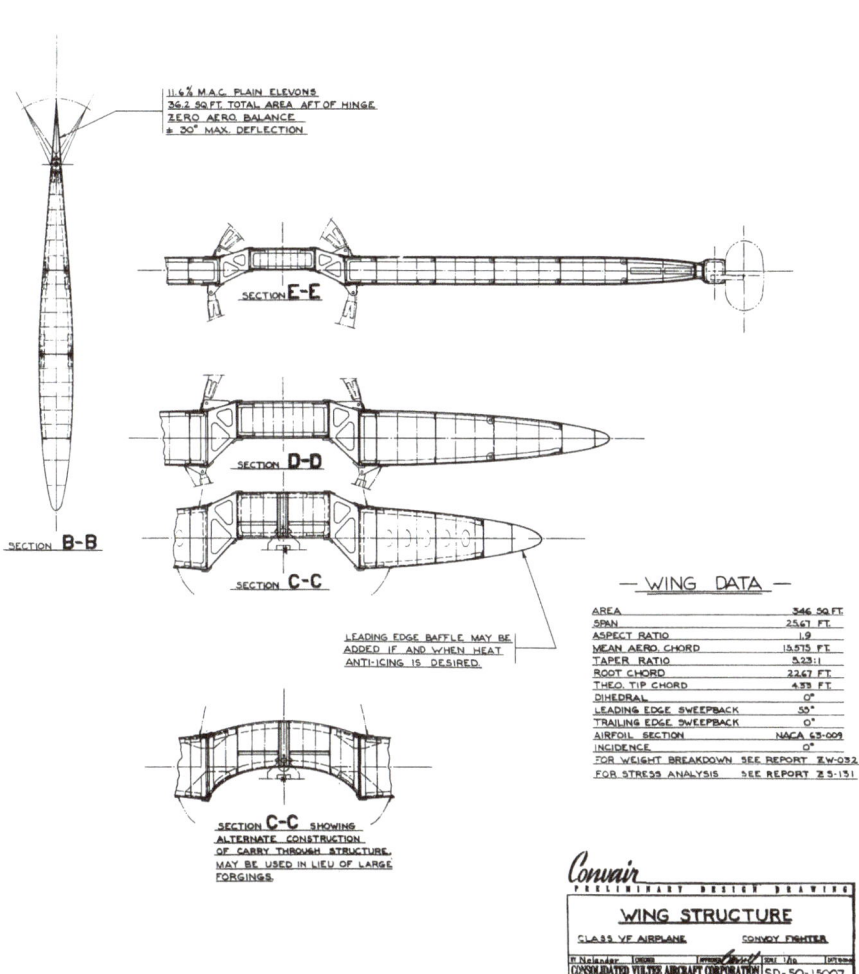

17) Schematic of the wing structure, which carried all the major loads, including the power plant, pilot's compartment, equipment and fin reactions.

18) Diagram of the Convoy Fighter's body structure. With the wing carrying the major loads, the fuselage was essentially non-structural, permitting the extensive use of large, quick opening doors and removable panels.

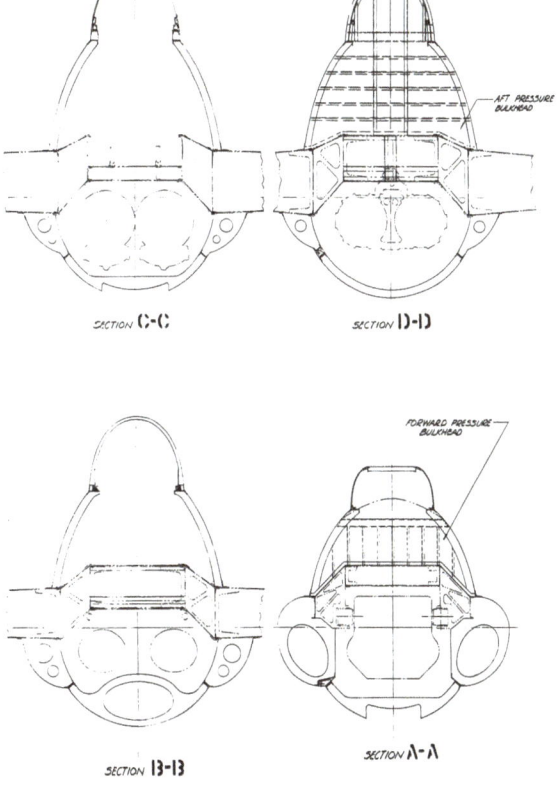

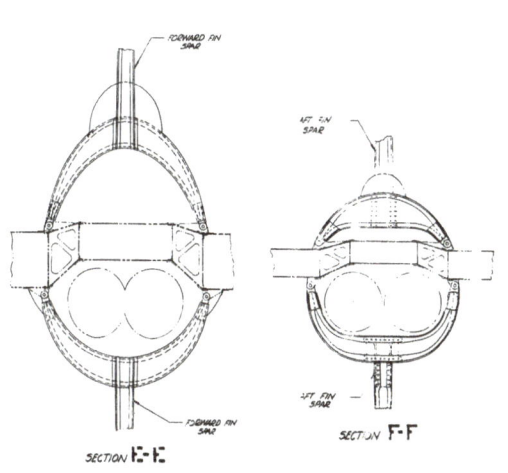

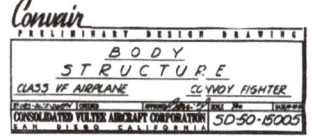

19) Blueprint of the vertical tail structure. Like the wing, the tail fins were of delta planform and had an inherent rigidity, resulting in a minimum of added structural weight to absorb the landing gear loads.

20) The landing gear installation consisted of four oleo struts mounted in faired pods at the tips of the wing and tail surfaces. An alternate landing gear with hard rubber tires is shown at the far left; this was what was actually used on the prototype XFY-1.

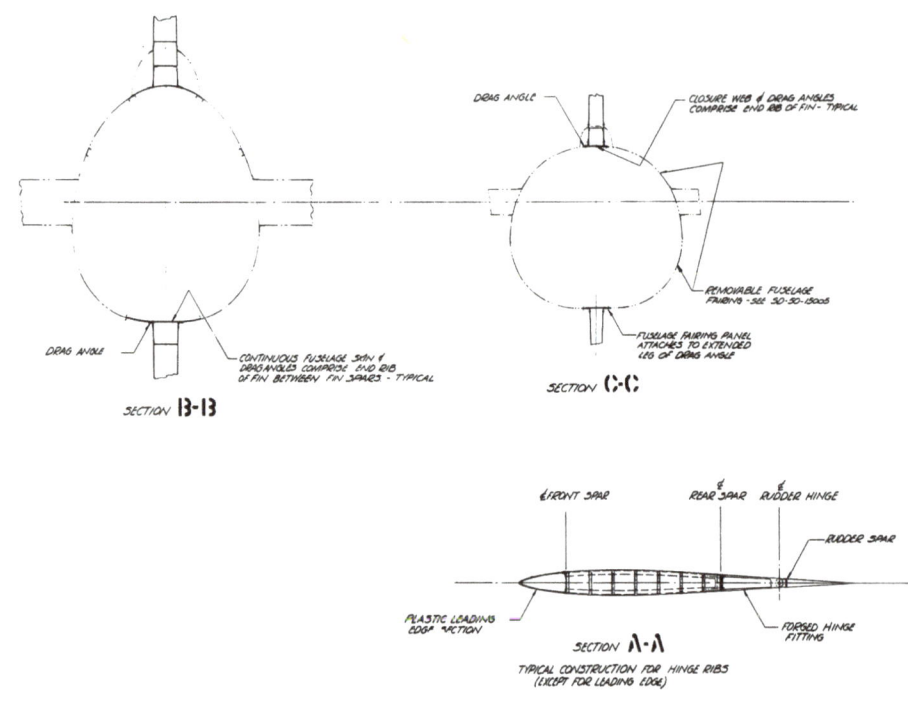

▲ 19 ▼ 20

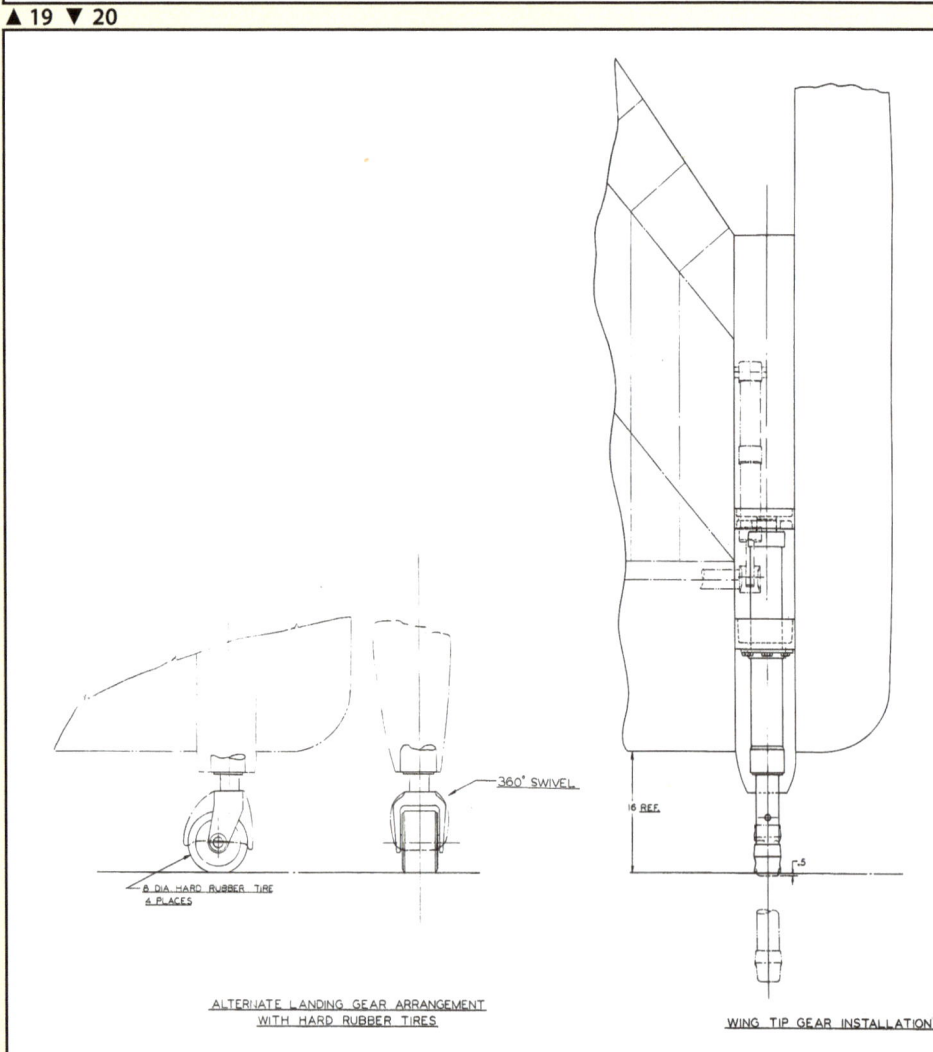

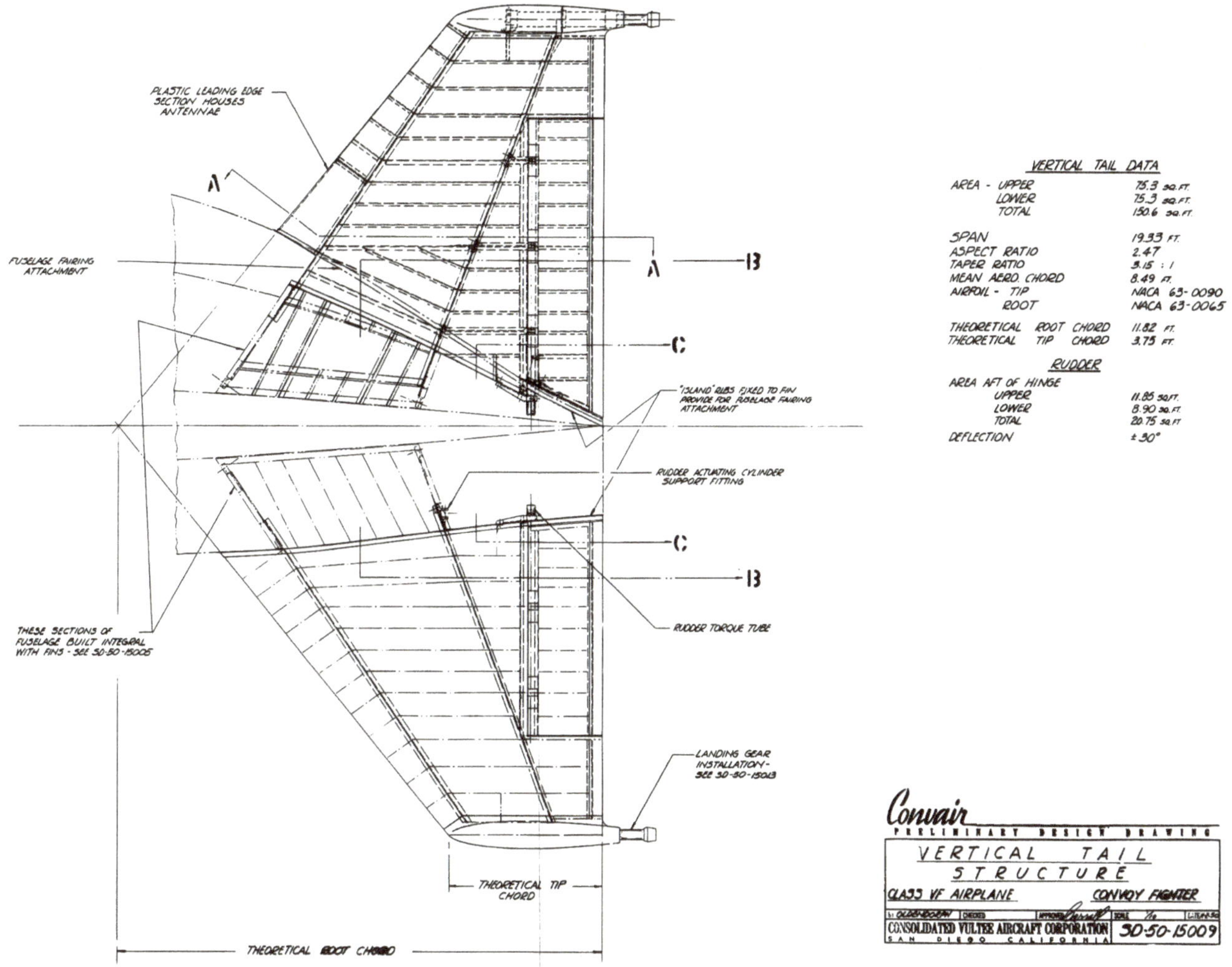
PLASTIC LEADING EDGE SECTION HOUSES ANTENNAE
FUSELAGE FAIRING ATTACHMENT
A'
A
B
C
"ISLAND" RIBS FIXED TO FIN PROVIDE FOR FUSELAGE FAIRING ATTACHMENT
RUDDER ACTUATING CYLINDER SUPPORT FITTING
RUDDER TORQUE TUBE
THESE SECTIONS OF FUSELAGE BUILT INTEGRAL WITH FINS - SEE SD-50-15005
LANDING GEAR INSTALLATION - SEE SD-50-15013
THEORETICAL TIP CHORD
THEORETICAL ROOT CHORD
VERTICAL TAIL DATA
AREA - UPPER 75.3 SQ.FT.
LOWER 75.3 SQ.FT.
TOTAL 150.6 SQ.FT.
SPAN 19.33 FT.
ASPECT RATIO 2.47
TAPER RATIO 3.15 : 1
MEAN AERO. CHORD 8.49 FT.
AIRFOIL - TIP NACA 63-0090
ROOT NACA 63-0065
THEORETICAL ROOT CHORD 11.82 FT.
THEORETICAL TIP CHORD 3.75 FT.
RUDDER
AREA AFT OF HINGE
UPPER 11.85 SQ.FT.
LOWER 8.90 SQ.FT.
TOTAL 20.75 SQ.FT
DEFLECTION ± 30°
Convair
PRELIMINARY DESIGN DRAWING
VERTICAL TAIL STRUCTURE
CLASS VF AIRPLANE
CONVOY FIGHTER
CONSOLIDATED VULTEE AIRCRAFT CORPORATION
SAN DIEGO CALIFORNIA
SD-50-15009

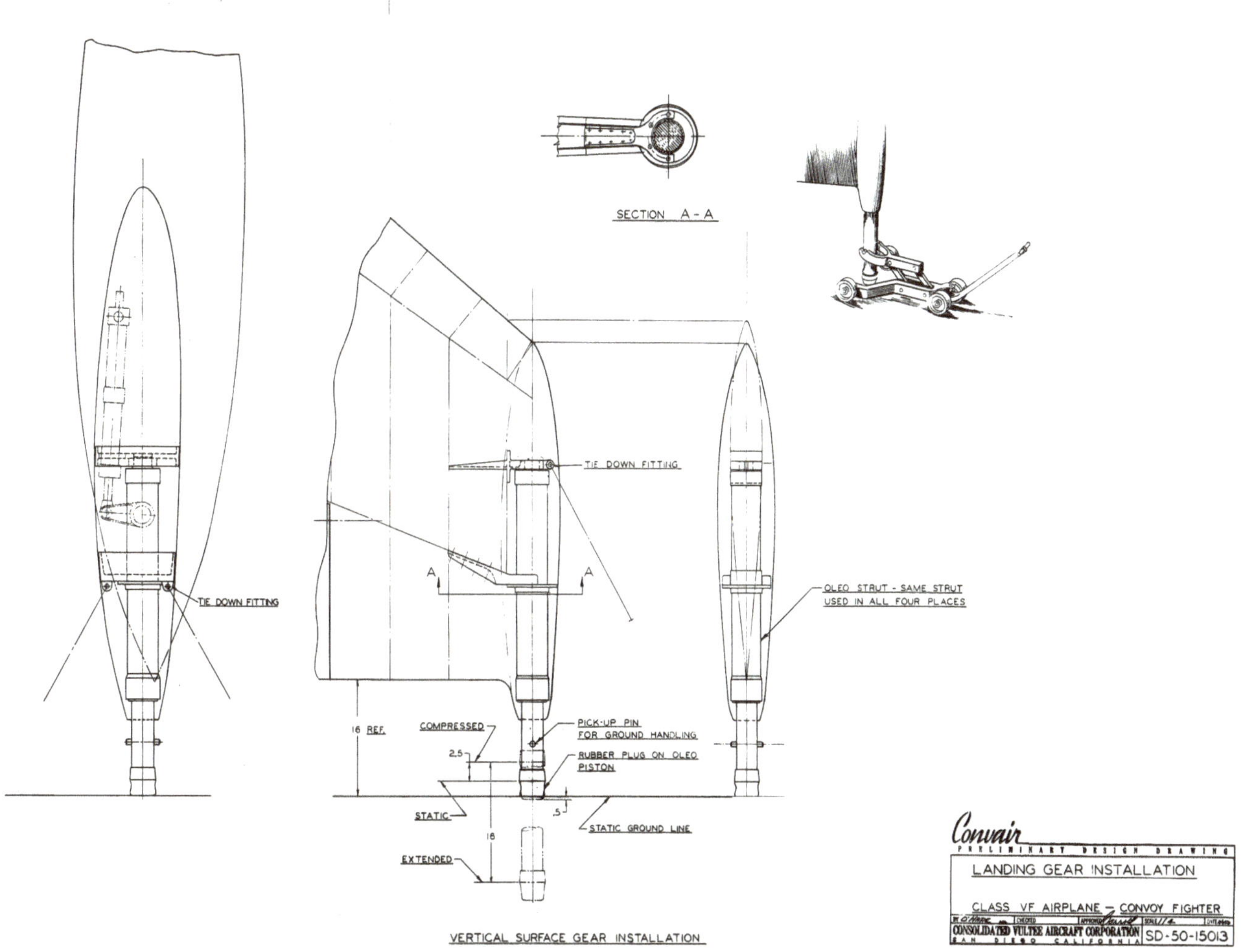
SECTION A - A
TIE DOWN FITTING
TIE DOWN FITTING
A
A
OLEO STRUT - SAME STRUT USED IN ALL FOUR PLACES
16 REF.
COMPRESSED
2.5
STATIC
16
EXTENDED
PICK-UP PIN FOR GROUND HANDLING
RUBBER PLUG ON OLEO PISTON
.5
STATIC GROUND LINE
VERTICAL SURFACE GEAR INSTALLATION
Convair
PRELIMINARY DESIGN DRAWING
LANDING GEAR INSTALLATION
CLASS VF AIRPLANE — CONVOY FIGHTER
CONSOLIDATED VULTEE AIRCRAFT CORPORATION
SAN DIEGO CALIFORNIA
SD-50-15013

WING T.E.
WING L.E.
FIN L.E.
FIN T.E.
PILOT'S EYE
CANOPY CONTROL LINE
CANOPY INTERSECTION
DUCT FAIRING CONTROL LINE
FUSELAGE CONTROL LINE (UPPER)
FUSELAGE CONTROL LINE (LOWER)
WING-FUSELAGE INTERSECTION
℄ THRUST
FILLET
LINE 'A'
LINE 'B'
LINE 'C'
STA 0
(REFERENCE LINE)
Convair
LINES
CLASS VF AIRPLANE

▲ 21 ▼ 22

ACCESS DOOR TO STARTER AIR CONNECTION & EXTERNAL POWER PLUG
AIR TURBINE TYPE STARTER USES OUTSIDE AIR PRESSURE SOURCE FOR STARTING ENGINE.
SECTION OF EACH INTAKE DUCT IS TAKEN OUT TO ALLOW FOR ENGINE REMOVAL
OIL TANK FILLER DOOR
FUEL TANK (REF.)
AFT ENGINE MT.
FIREWALL
AFT FUEL BOOSTER PUMP IN SUMP TANK
℄ THRUST
℄ TURBINE & TAILPIPE
℄ TURBINE & TAILPIPE
OIL TANK
AIR INTAKE DUCT SHUTOFF DOOR
ENGINE AIR INTAKE DUCT
SEE DETAIL F FOR AUXILIARY AIR DOOR
FWD FUEL BOOSTER PUMP IN SUMP TANK
SEE DETAIL F FOR SHAFT FAIRING
FLUSH TYPE INTAKES FOR BURNER COMPARTMENT COOLING AIR
SHROUD
INSULATING BLANKET
FUEL TANK (REF) SEE WING STRUCTURE DWG. SD-50-15007
PLAN VIEW
℄ PROP
℄ PROP
A
B
C
SPEED SHIFT SECTION ADDED TO GEARBOX
OIL TANK (PRESSURIZED TYPE WITH BLADDER TO ALLOW OPERATION IN ANY FLIGHT ATTITUDE)
ALLISON T40-A-8 ENGINE
FWD ENGINE MTS
GENERATOR
STARTER
FWD FUEL BOOSTER PUMP IN SUMP TANK
SHROUD
ACCESSORY COMPARTMENT
AFT ENGINE MT.
FIREWALL SEPARATING BURNER COMPARTMENT FROM ACCESSORY COMPARTMENT
SHROUD
INSULATING BLANKET
AFT FUEL BOOSTER PUMP IN SUMP TANK
TWIN CIRCULAR TAILPIPES OF EJECTOR TYPE AUGMENT COOLING AIRFLOW
℄ THRUST
BELLMOUTHS
PNEUMATICALLY DRIVEN ALTERNATOR MOUNTED ON ENGINE REMOVAL DOOR
FLUSH SCOOP FOR OIL COOLER AIR
OIL COOLER AIR EXIT DUCT
OIL COOLER MOUNTED ON ENGINE REMOVAL DOOR
COMPRESSOR BLEED AIR NOZZLES (2) USED TO AUGMENT OIL COOLER AIRFLOW FOR GROUND OPERATION & HOVERING FLIGHT
OIL COOLER AIR EXIT FLAP
BURNER COMPARTMENT
ENGINE REMOVAL DOOR LENGTH
SIDE VIEW

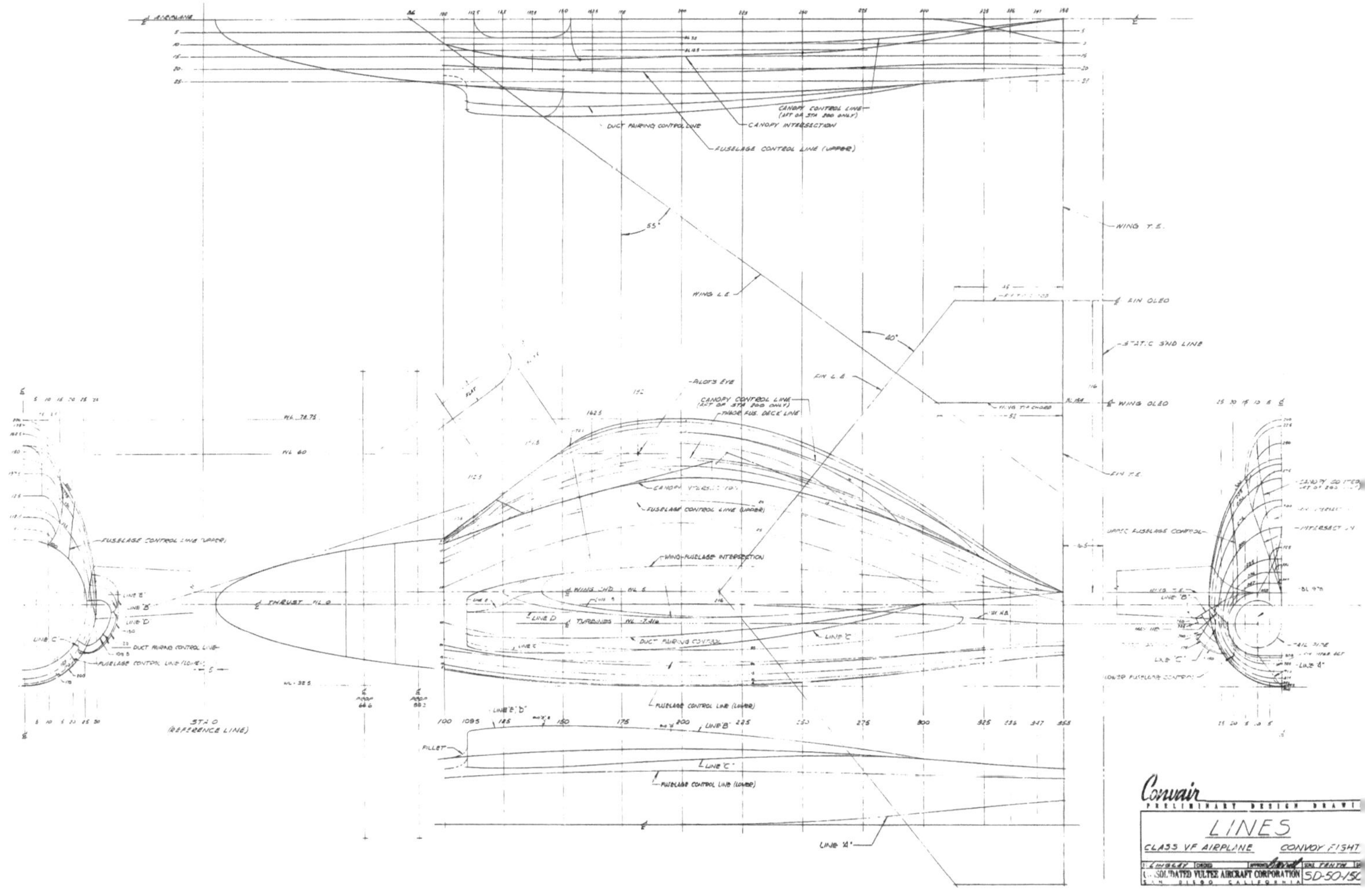

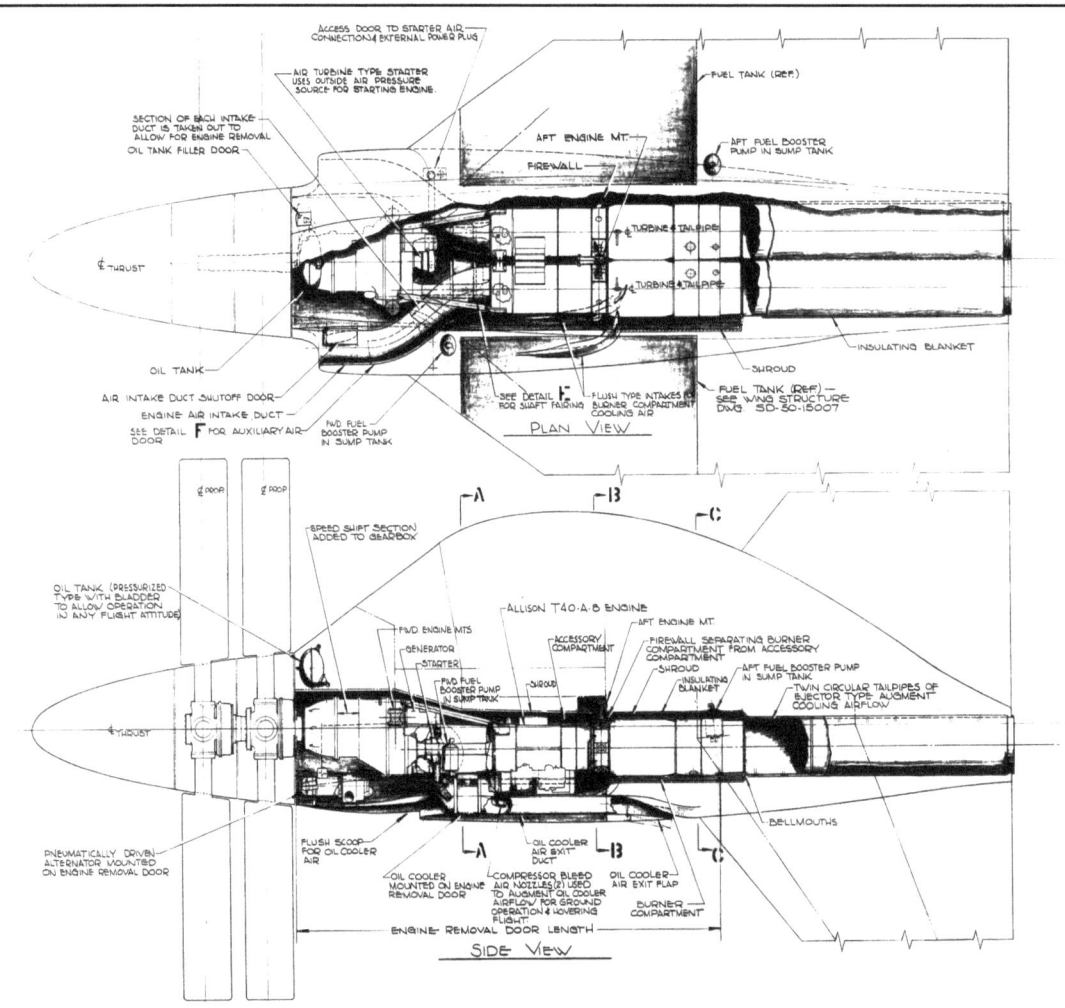

21) Fuselage loft lines of the Convair Class VF Convoy Fighter.

22) Blueprint of the Allison T40-A-8 turboprop engine installation.

23) Diagram of the control system; all controls were power operated.

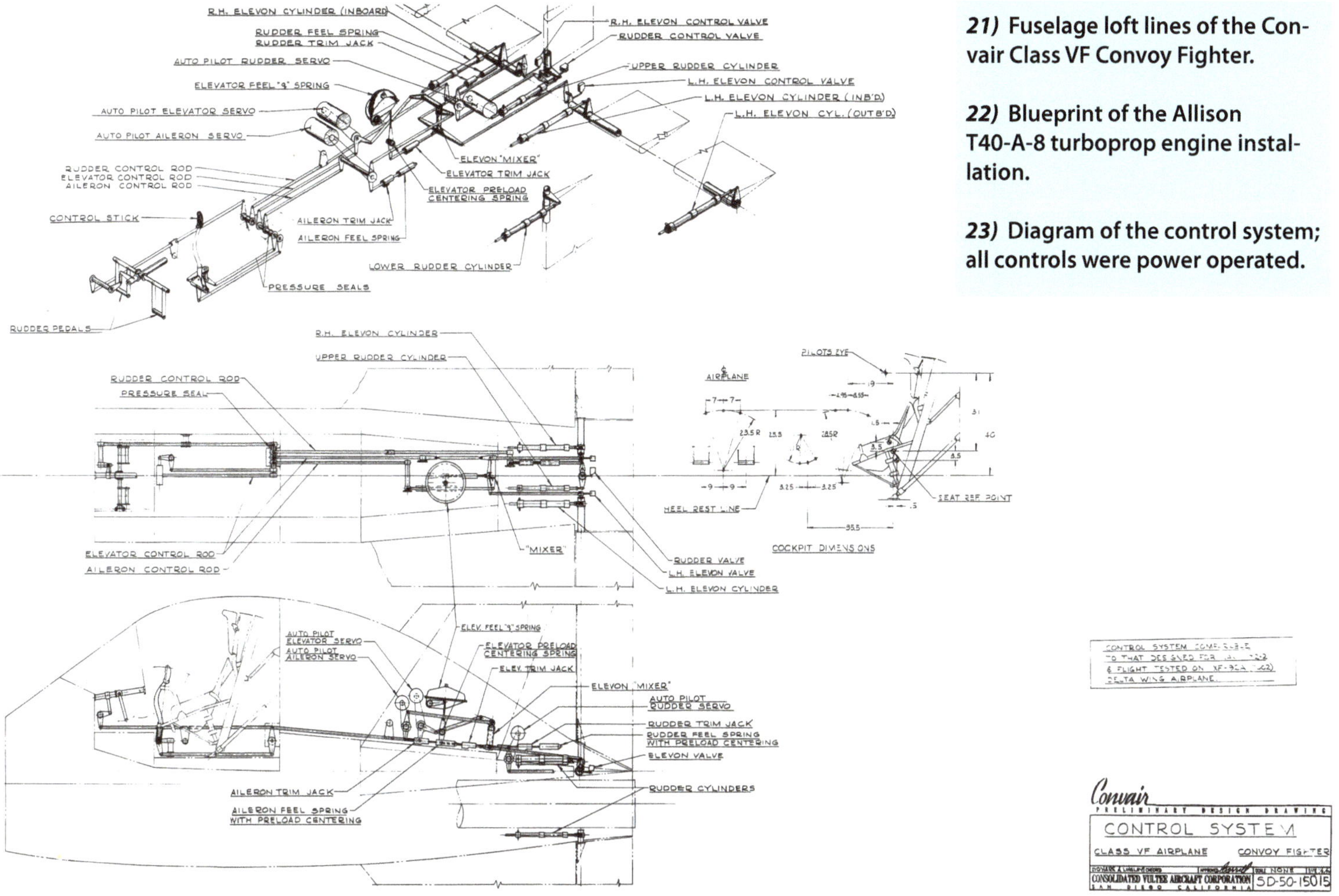

▲ 23

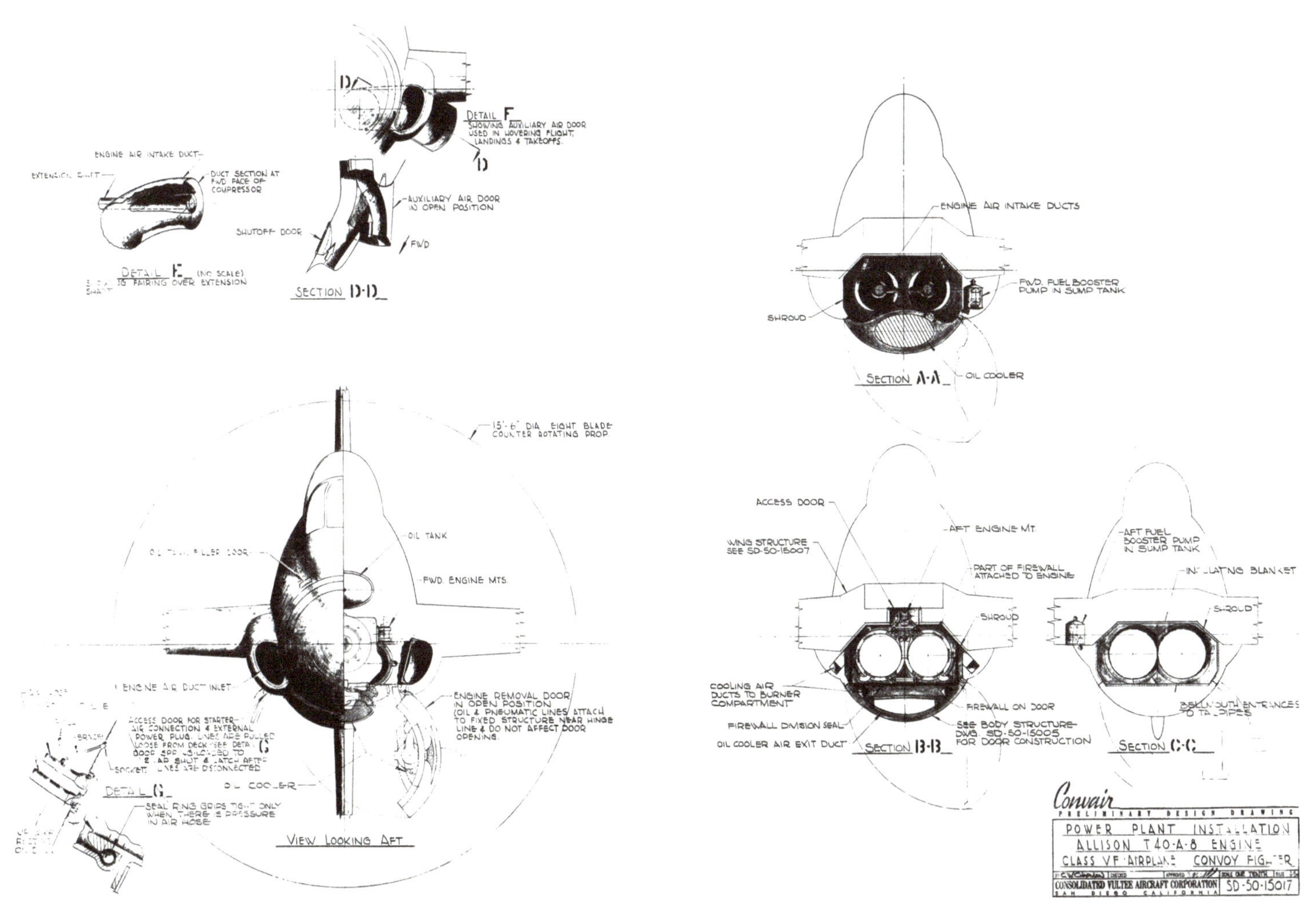

24) Four 20 mm Mk. 12 Mod. 0 (T118) fixed aircraft guns, with 150 rounds each, could be installed in pairs at the wing tips of the Convair Convoy Fighter.

25) An alternate armament installation consisted of fifty 2.75" folding fin rockets—twenty-five in each wing tip fairing. Each fairing was divided into three parts, with the front and aft portions being released prior to firing, and the central section containing the tubes being released afterwards.

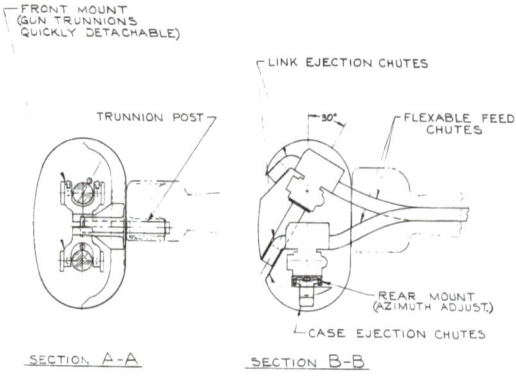

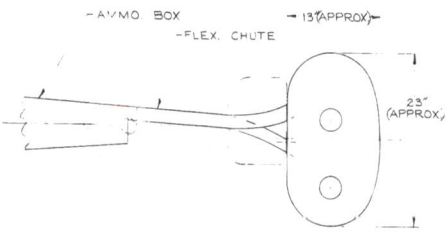

▲ 24 ▼ 25

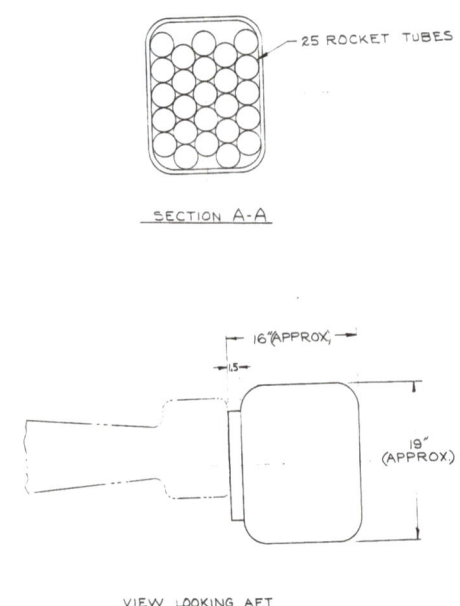

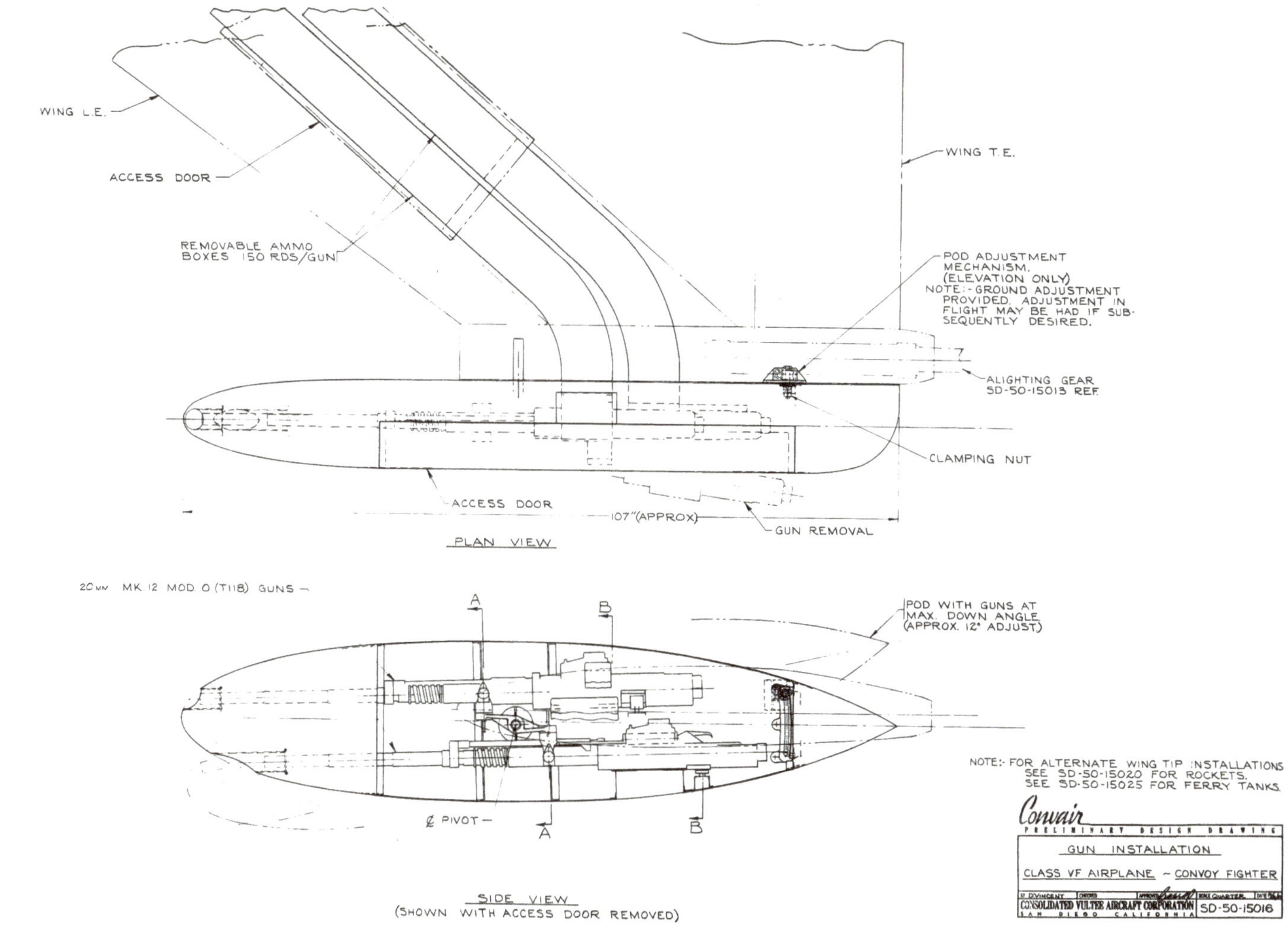
WING L.E.
ACCESS DOOR
REMOVABLE AMMO BOXES 150 RDS/GUN
WING T.E.
POD ADJUSTMENT MECHANISM. (ELEVATION ONLY)
NOTE:- GROUND ADJUSTMENT PROVIDED. ADJUSTMENT IN FLIGHT MAY BE HAD IF SUBSEQUENTLY DESIRED.
ALIGHTING GEAR SD-50-15013 REF.
CLAMPING NUT
ACCESS DOOR
107"(APPROX)
GUN REMOVAL
PLAN VIEW
20MM MK.12 MOD 0 (T118) GUNS
A
B
POD WITH GUNS AT MAX. DOWN ANGLE (APPROX. 12° ADJUST)
℄ PIVOT
A
B
NOTE:- FOR ALTERNATE WING TIP INSTALLATIONS SEE SD-50-15020 FOR ROCKETS. SEE SD-50-15025 FOR FERRY TANKS.
Convair
PRELIMINARY DESIGN DRAWING
GUN INSTALLATION
CLASS VF AIRPLANE ~ CONVOY FIGHTER
CONSOLIDATED VULTEE AIRCRAFT CORPORATION
SAN DIEGO CALIFORNIA
SD-50-15016
SIDE VIEW (SHOWN WITH ACCESS DOOR REMOVED)

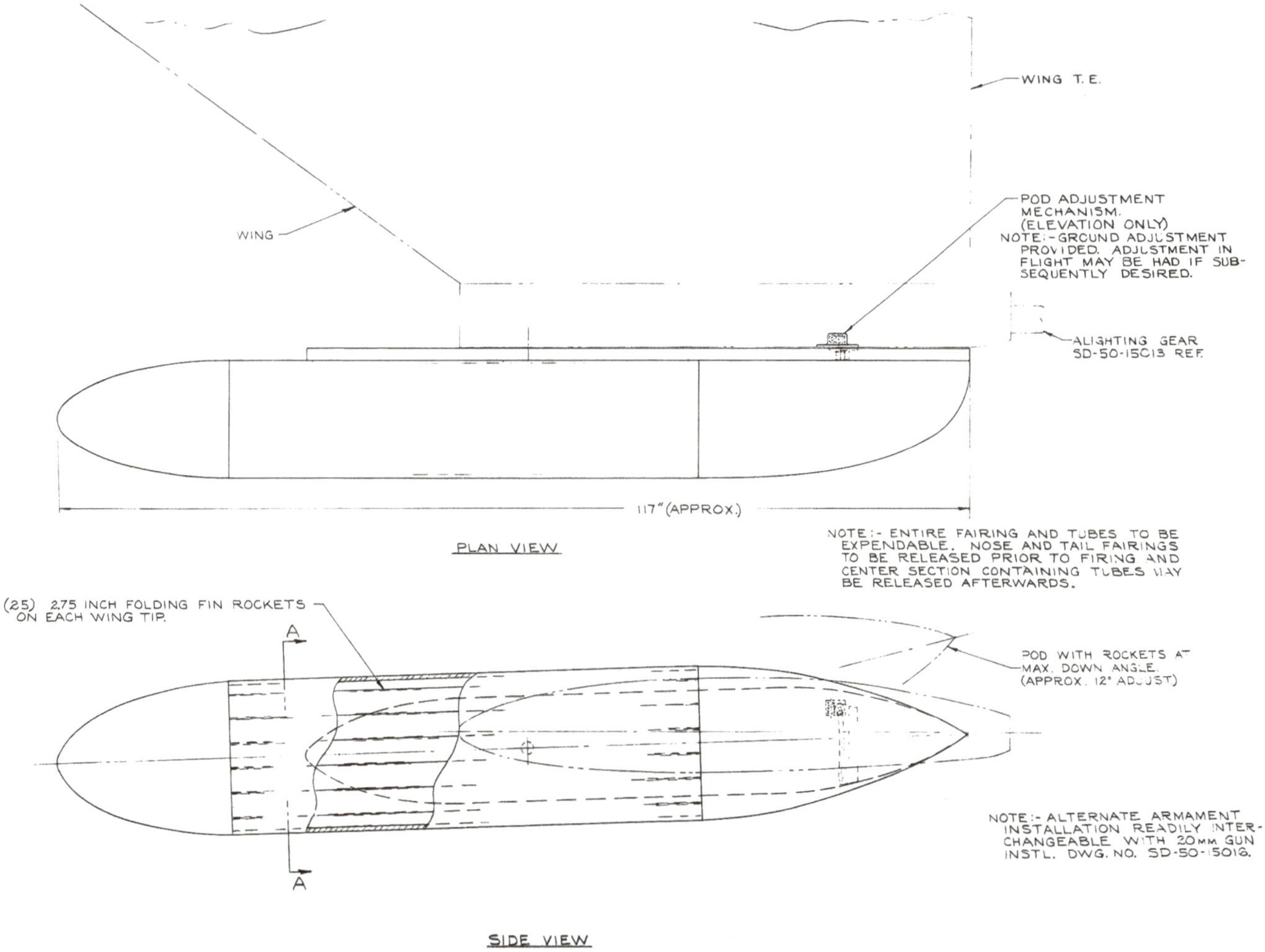
WING T.E.
WING
POD ADJUSTMENT MECHANISM. (ELEVATION ONLY)
NOTE:- GROUND ADJUSTMENT PROVIDED. ADJUSTMENT IN FLIGHT MAY BE HAD IF SUBSEQUENTLY DESIRED.
ALIGHTING GEAR SD-50-15013 REF.
117"(APPROX.)
PLAN VIEW
NOTE:- ENTIRE FAIRING AND TUBES TO BE EXPENDABLE. NOSE AND TAIL FAIRINGS TO BE RELEASED PRIOR TO FIRING AND CENTER SECTION CONTAINING TUBES MAY BE RELEASED AFTERWARDS.
(25) 2.75 INCH FOLDING FIN ROCKETS ON EACH WING TIP.
A
POD WITH ROCKETS AT MAX. DOWN ANGLE. (APPROX. 12° ADJUST)
NOTE:- ALTERNATE ARMAMENT INSTALLATION READILY INTERCHANGEABLE WITH 20MM GUN INSTL. DWG. NO. SD-50-15016.
A
SIDE VIEW

26) Another alternative to the gun installation was a pair of 500 lb (approximately 85 gallon) fuel tanks mounted on the wing tips for ferrying purposes.

27) Assembly diagram of the Convoy Class VF Convoy Fighter proposal.

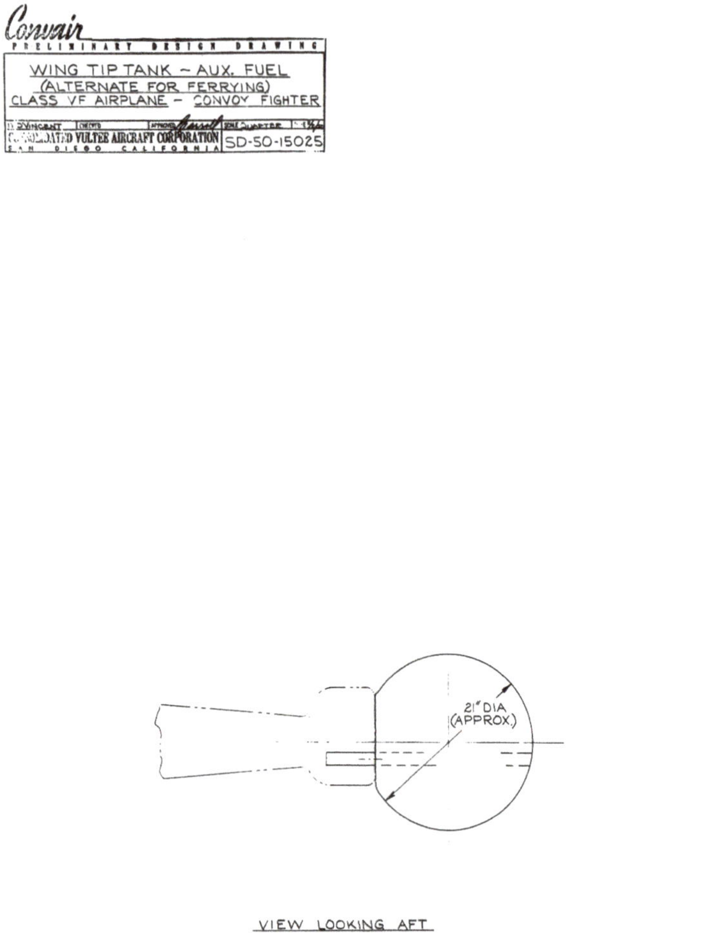

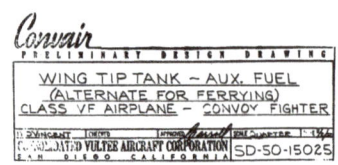
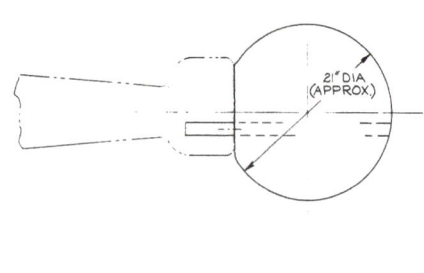

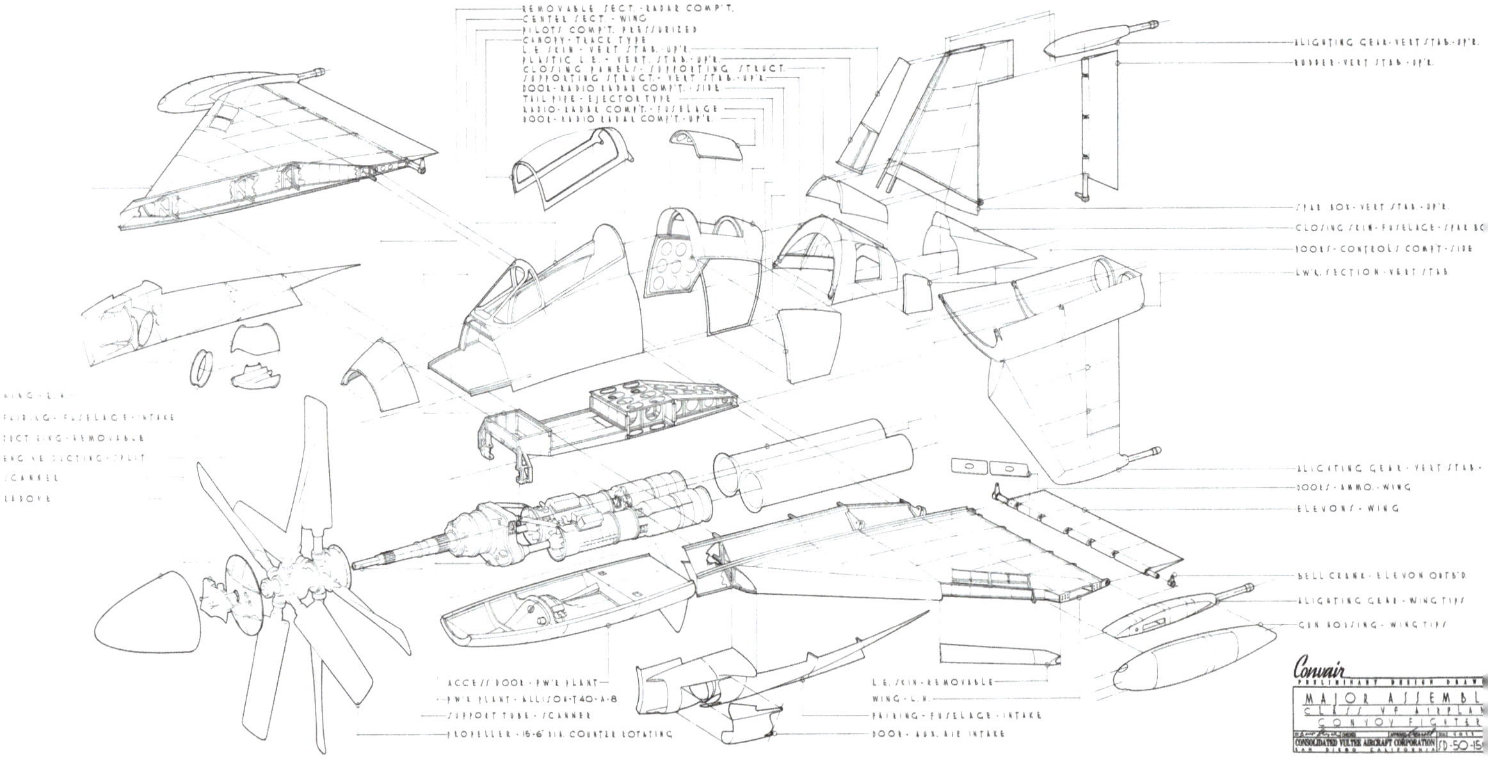

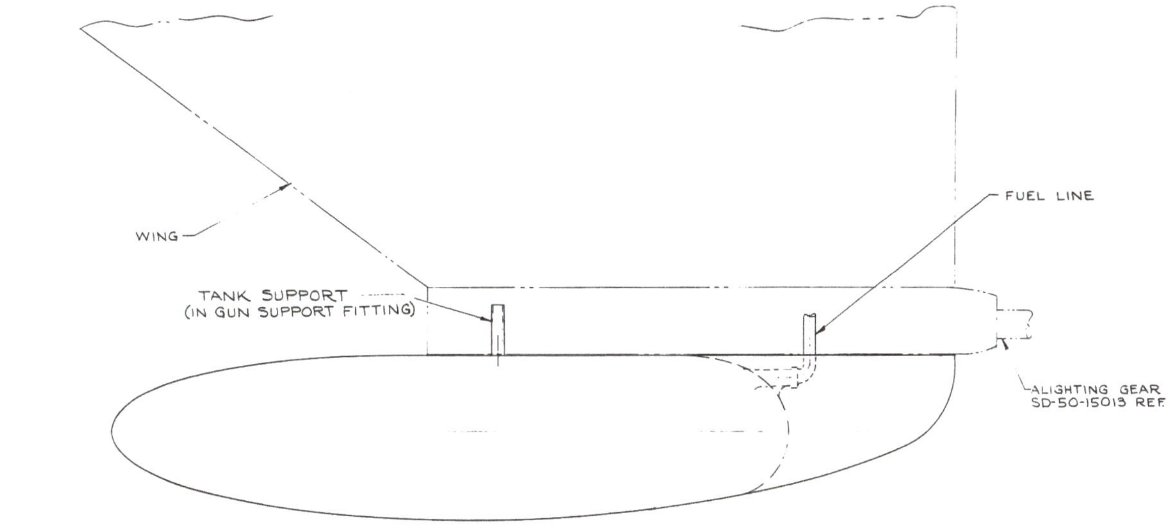

PLAN VIEW

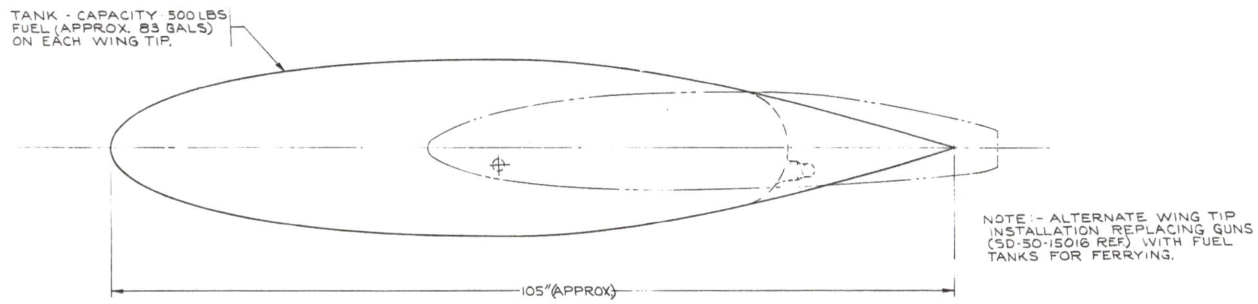

SIDE VIEW

Other Publications by Jared A. Zichek

Books from Retromechanix Productions

Available from Amazon & other booksellers

Streamlined Dreams: Ten Amazing Unbuilt Automobile Designs, 1916-1939 Ninety-four color illos of strange & beautiful auto projects of the interwar era; 102 pp. **Print $21.99/Digital $9.99**

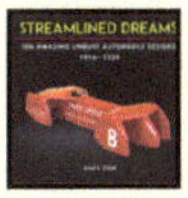

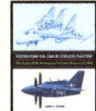

Goodyear GA-28A/B *Convoy Fighter*: The Naval VTOL Turboprop Tailsitter Project of 1950 Forty illos of a bizarre competitor to the Convair Pogo & Lockheed Salmon; 34 pp. **Print $14.99/Digital $5.99**

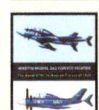

Martin Model 262 *Convoy Fighter*: The Naval VTOL Turboprop Project of 1950 Fifty-six illos of Martin's proposed rivals to the Convair Pogo & Lockheed Salmon; 52 pp. **Print $16.99/Digital $6.99**

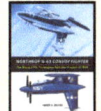

Northrop N-63 *Convoy Fighter*: The Naval VTOL Turboprop Tailsitter Project of 1950 Sixty-six illos of Northrop's handsome VTOL fighter proposals; 44 pp. **Print $15.99/Digital $6.49**

The American Aerospace Archive Magazine

Available at magcloud.com/user/jaredzichek

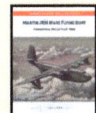

1. Martin JRM Mars Flying Boat: Commercial Projects of 1944 Reproduction of a beautiful full color brochure for a civilian version of the world's largest flying boat; 36 pp. **Print $9.95/Digital $3.95**

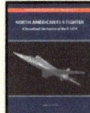

2. North American FJ-5 Fighter: A Navalized Derivative of the F-107A Five wind tunnel model photos and 28 drawings of North American's unusual 1955 proposal; 36 pp. **Print $9.95/Digital $3.95**

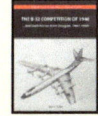

3. The B-52 Competition of 1946...and Dark Horses from Douglas, 1947-1950 Seventy-seven rare images of early postwar strategic bomber projects; 60 pp. **Print $14.95/Digital $5.95**

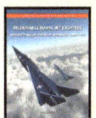

4. McDonnell Naval Jet Fighters: Selected Proposals and Mock-up Reports, 1945-1957 97 photos and drawings of early postwar jet fighter proposals & prototypes; 60 pp. **Print $14.95/Digital $5.95**

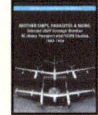

5. Mother Ships, Parasites and More: Selected USAF Strategic Bomber, XC Heavy Transport and FICON Studies, 1945-1954 Composite aircraft projects; 258 illos; 204 pp. **Print $49.95/Digital $9.95**

Books from Schiffer Publishing

Available from Amazon & other booksellers

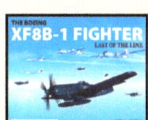

The Boeing XF8B-1 Fighter: Last of the Line Hundreds of rare photos, drawings, artist's impressions and manual extracts covering Boeing's last piston engine fighter; 376 pp. **$45.59**

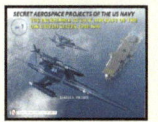

Secret Aerospace Projects of the U.S. Navy: The Incredible Attack Aircraft of the USS United States, 1948-1949 Hundreds of rare photos and drawings; 232 pp. **$45.81**

Websites

RETRO MECHANIX *Yesterday's Wings of Tomorrow*

Retromechanix.com features hundreds of rare high resolution images and reports covering U.S. prototype and project aircraft from the 1930s through the 1950s. Many free and low cost digital downloads available!

CLASS VF AIRPLANE PROTOTYPE FOR CONVOY FIGHTER

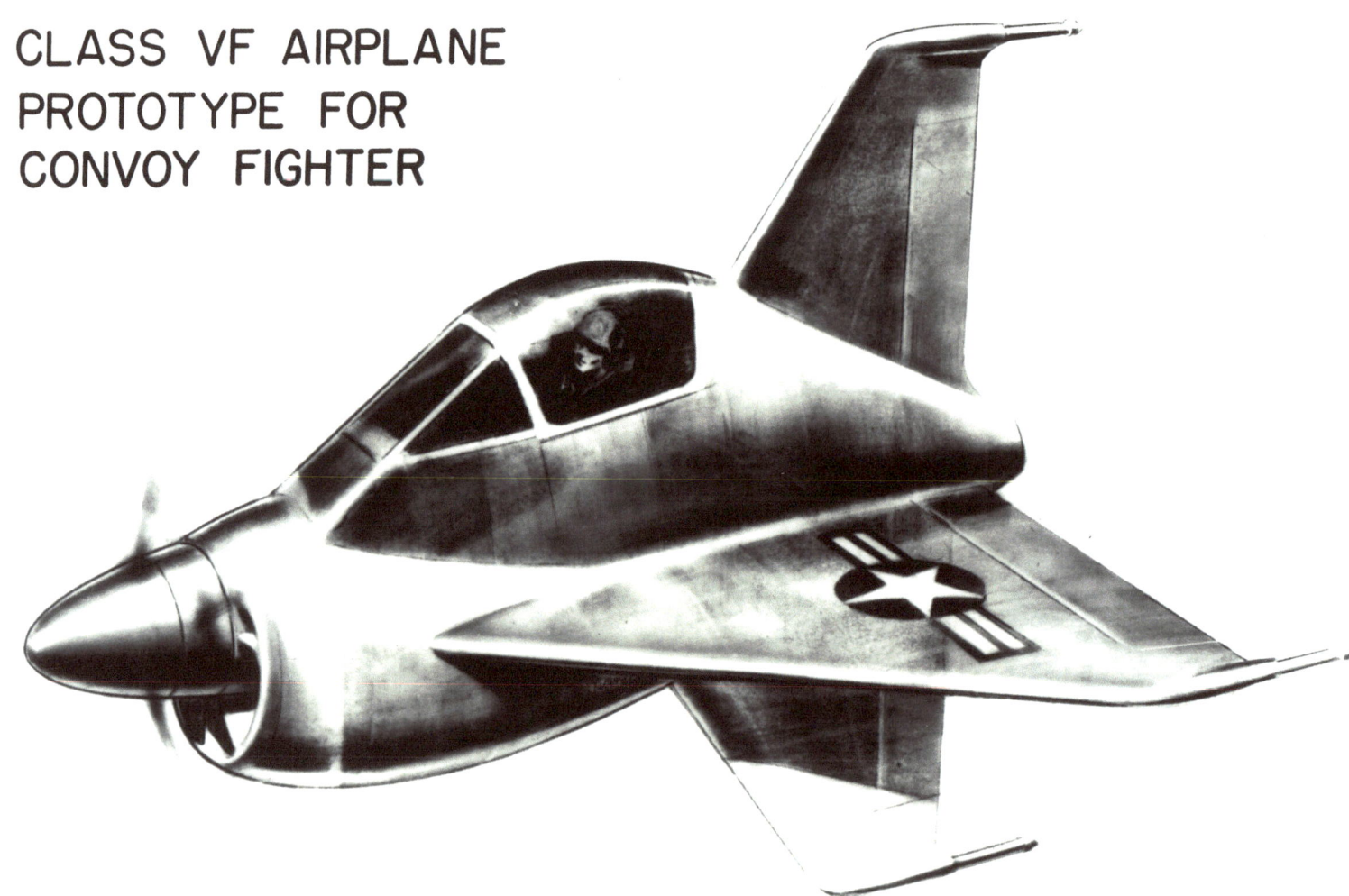

▲ 28

Class VF Airplane Prototype for Convoy Fighter

As per the original OS-122 requirement, Convair designed and submitted a proposal for 0.766 scale prototype of the Convoy Fighter to serve as a technology demonstrator. This prototype was intended for use in the investigation of vertical takeoff and landing and other flight characteristics as part of the development program for the Convoy Fighter.

The prototype airplane was a one-place, flyable, unpressurized dimensionally and dynamically similar 0.766 scale prototype of the Convoy Fighter. This airplane was capable of vertical, unassisted takeoffs from and landings on small platform areas.

The airplane had a delta wing and both an upper and lower vertical tail surface, also of delta configuration. Control surfaces were power operated. The airplane was provided with a Navy standard ejection seat which could be rotated through 45° for vision in the vertical attitude.

Alighting gear was provided on the tips of the wing and vertical tail surfaces. An auxiliary, conventional landing gear was provided for test purposes. The airplane was powered by a dual rotating propeller driven by a Armstrong Siddeley Double Mamba III turboprop engine.

Like the other manufacturers participating in the Convoy Fighter competition, Convair advised BuAer to save money by forgoing the construction of the 0.766 scale prototype and building instead a stripped version of the full-scale Convoy Fighter with a less powerful turboprop engine. This proposal is covered in the next section.

28) Artist's impression of the Convair's 0.766 scale prototype of the Convoy Fighter, designed to meet the original OS-122 requirement.

29) Three-view and fuel tank diagram taken from the Standard Aircraft Characteristics (SAC) charts prepared for the type.

30) Another general arrangement of the prototype, this one included in correspondence from Convair to BuAer.

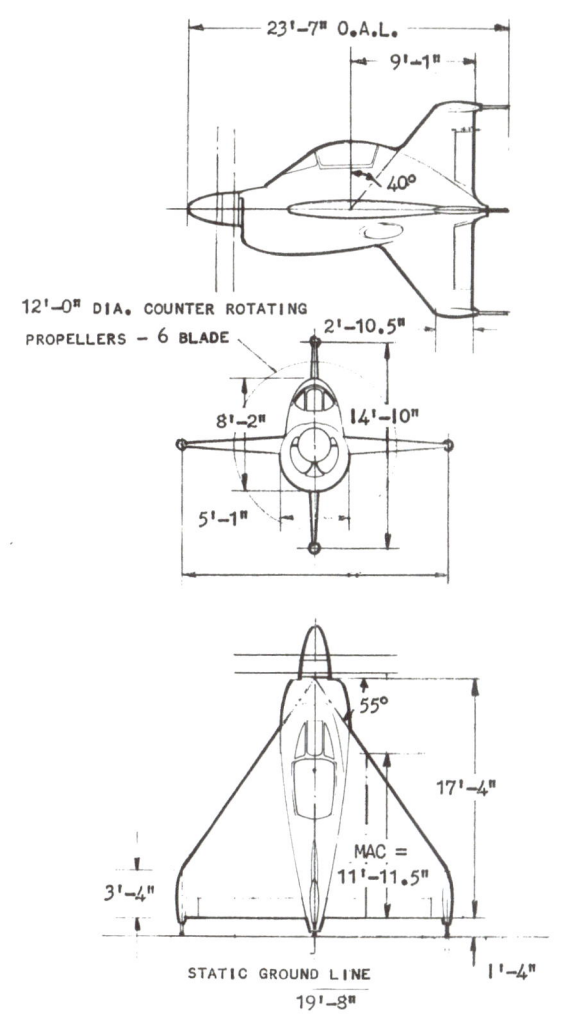
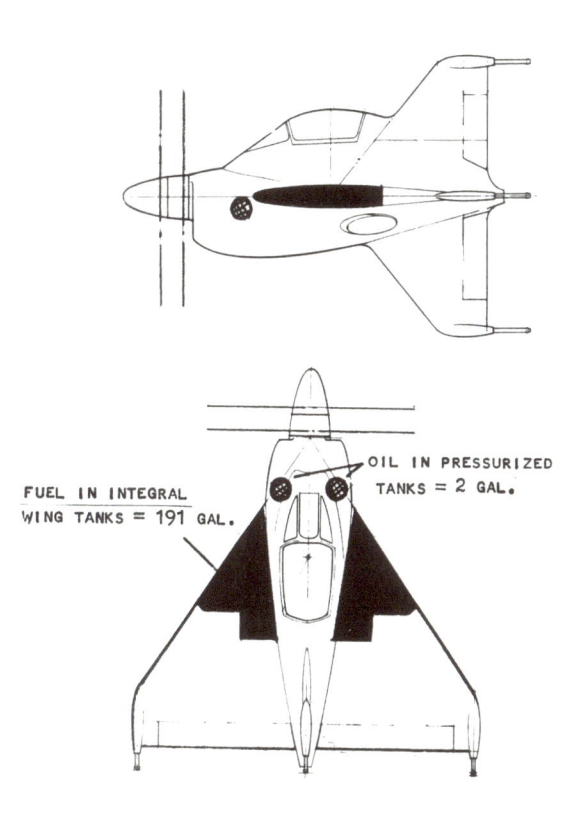

PROTOTYPE FOR
CONVOY FIGHTER

DATE: NOV. 1, 50

CONVAIR
SAN DIEGO, CALIFORNIA

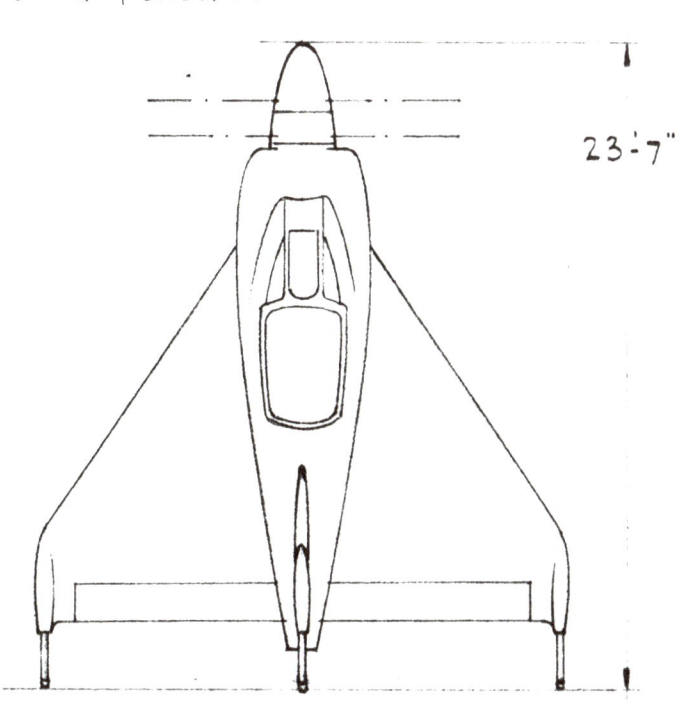
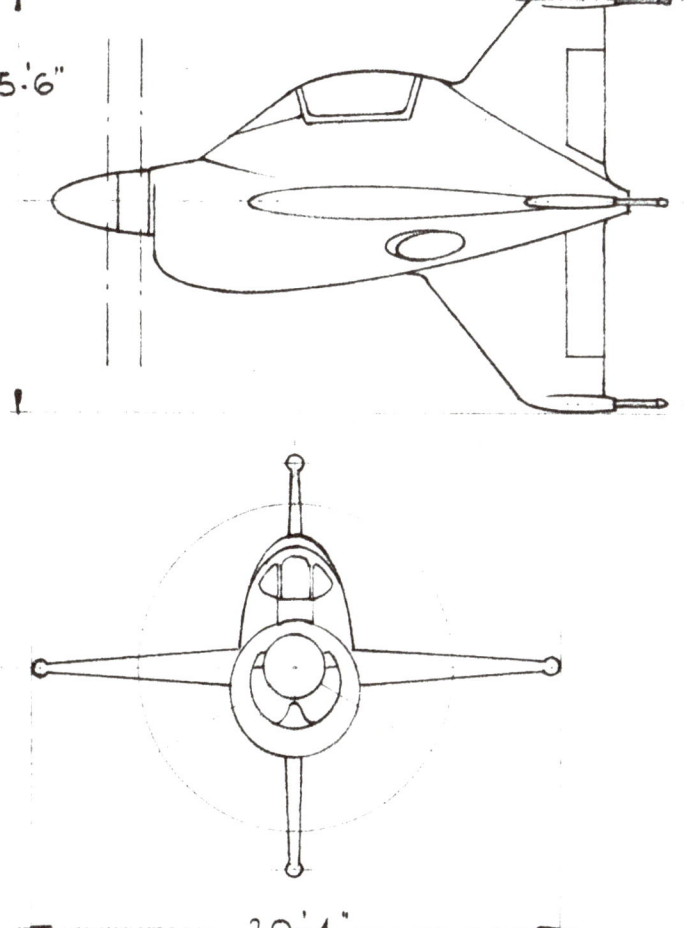

PROPOSAL

MISSION AND DESCRIPTION

MISSION:
This airplane is intended as a prototype for the Convoy Fighter presented in Report ZP-50-15002 and corresponding Standard Aircraft Characteristics Charts.

DESCRIPTION

The prototype airplane is a one-place, flyable, dimensionally and dynamically similar 0.766 scale prototype of the Convoy Fighter. This airplane is capable of vertical, unassisted take-off from and landing on, small platform areas.

The airplane has a delta wing and both an upper and lower vertical tail surface, also of delta configuration. Control surfaces are power operated. The airplane is provided with a Navy standard ejection seat which may be rotated through 45° for vision in the vertical attitude.

Alighting gear is provided on the tips of the wing and vertical tail surfaces. An auxiliary, conventional landing gear is provided for test purposes. The airplane is powered by a dual rotating propeller driven by a turbo-prop engine.

WEIGHTS

	G.W.	L.F.
Empty	5982	–
Basic	6070	–
Design	7008	+7.5*
Max. T.O.	7500	
(Limited by min. flight accel. during take-off – spec. OS-121)		
Max. Landing	6762	+3.0**

* Limit maneuver L.F.
** Limited by alighting gear deflection

FUEL AND OIL

LOCATION	CAPACITY
Wing	191 Gal.

Tanks are integral – not self sealing – fuel conforms to Spec MIL-F-5616 (JP-1)

OIL

LOCATION	CAPACITY
Fuselage (2 separ. tanks)	2 Gal.

Oil conforms to Spec. AN-03 – Grade M

POWER PLANT

ENGINE: 1 Armstrong-Siddeley "Double Mamba" Turbo-Prop Model ASMD-1, as per engine spec., issue #3, March 1950; Length 79.83", Height 43.85", Width 52.8" – Propeller: six-blade-dual-12' dia., activity factor = 150, design C_{ℓ_i} = 0.50 Reduction gear – 10.3:1

RATINGS

	RPM	PROP SHP	JET THRUST (LB)
T.O.	15000	2640	810
Max.Cont. Cruise	14500	2095	710

Per Eng.Spec. Issue#3 March 1950

ORDNANCE

NONE

DIMENSIONS

Wing Span	19'8"
Fuselage Length	22'2"
Vert. Tail Span	14'10"
Wing Area	203 sq.ft.
Wing MAC	11'11.5"
Wing A.R.	1.9
Wing L.E. Sweep	55°

ELECTRONICS

AN/ARC-27   UHF
AN/APN-1   Radio Altimeter

NOVEMBER 1950 — CONVAIR — CONVOY FIGHTER PROTOTYPE

PROPOSAL

PERFORMANCE SUMMARY

LOADING CONDITION		FLIGHT TEST
Take-off Weight	lbs.	7500
Fuel	lbs.	1230
Bombs		0
Wing/Power Loading (A) lbs/sq.ft; lbs/bhp		36.9/2.53
Stall Speed--Power off	kn.	
Stall Speed--Power off - No Fuel	kn.	NOT APPLICABLE
Stall Speed--Power on	kn.	
Maximum Speed/Alt (B)	kn/ft.	518/S.L.
Take-off Distance, deck -- calm	ft.	0
Take-off Distance, deck	kn.	0
Take-off Distance, Airport	ft.	0
Rate of climb -- sea level (B)	ft/min.	10,800
Service Ceiling (RC=100 FPM)(B)	ft.	43,000
Time-to-climb 20000 ft. (B)(C)	min.	3.11
Time-to-climb 35000 ft. (B)(C)(D)	min.	7.81
Combat Range/V av	ft. n.mi/kn.	NOT APPLICABLE (SEE NOTE H)
Combat Radius/V av	ft. n.mi/kn.	NOT APPLICABLE (SEE NOTE H)
LOADING CONDITION		FLT DES. G.W.
Gross Weight	lbs.	7008
Engine power		MAXIMUM
Fuel	lbs.	738
Bombs/Tanks		0
Max. speed at sea level	kn.	520
Max. speed/Alt	kn/ft.	520/S.L.
Max. Speed/35000 (D)	kn/ft.	495
Rate of climb SL	ft/min.	11,700
Ceiling for 500 fpm R/C	ft.	42,500
Time-to-climb/Alt.	min/ft.	7.0/35000

NOTES

(A) BHP at Maximum Critical Altitude (take-off power @ .SL.)
(B) Military Power
(C) From standing start
(D) Exception from MIL-C-5011
(E) Performance is based on calculations using wind tunnel tests in correlation with flight test results and NACA reports on an airplane of similar planform, NACA standard atmosphere
(F) Fuel consumption is based on engine specification fuel consumption data using fuel of 6.7 #/gal density
(G) Fuel consumption data are increased 5%
(H) Endurance at Sea Level for flight test is as follows:
At reduced power (300 kn airspeed)-68 min.
At take-off power (520 kn airspeed)-24 min.
At reduced power after fuel allowed for 10 min warm-up, take-off and landing at take-off power (300 knots airspeed) – 45 min.

NOVEMBER 1950 — CONVAIR — CONVOY FIGHTER PROTOTYPE

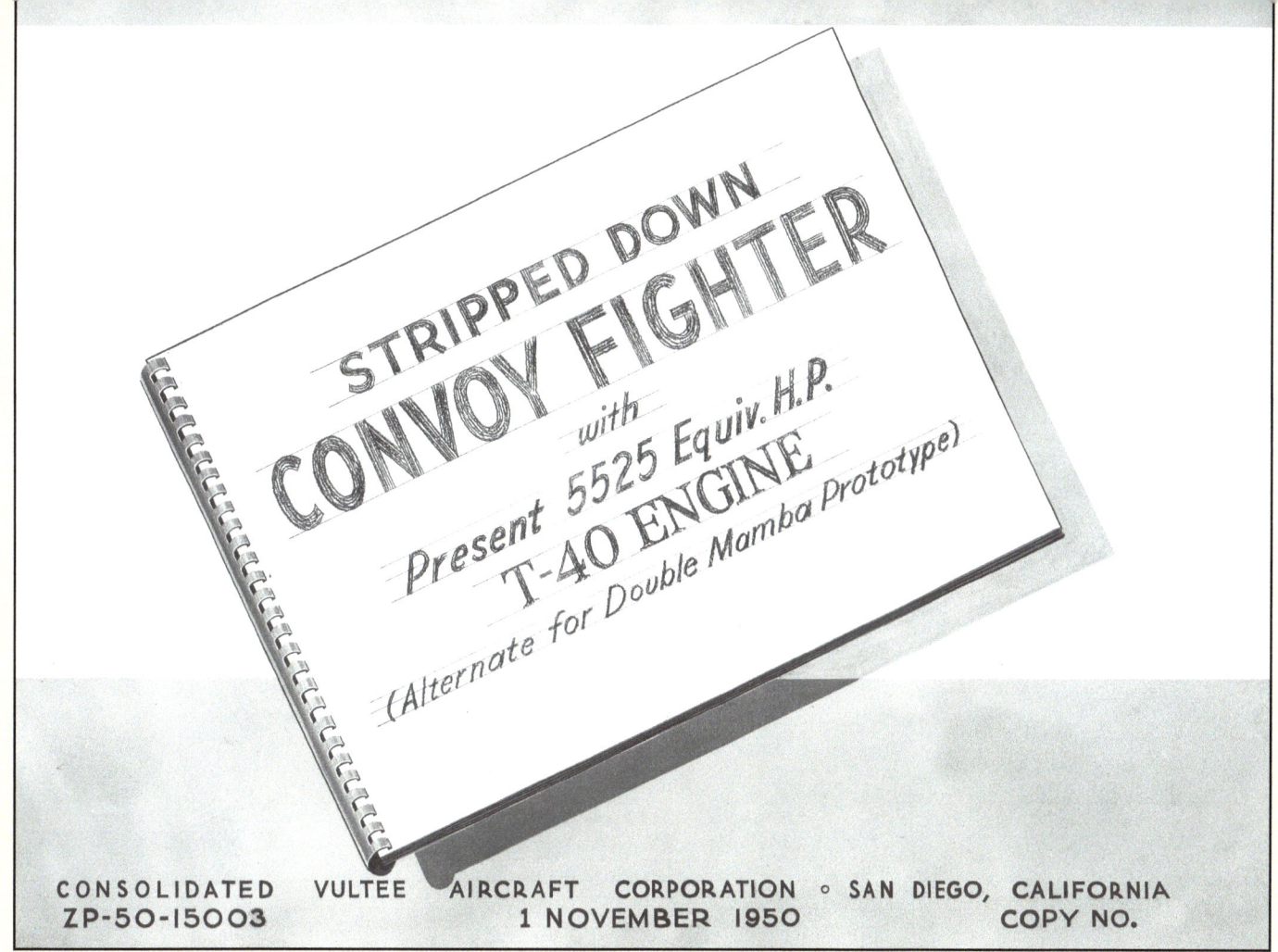

Stripped Down Convoy Fighter

An alternative to building the 0.766 scale prototype was the construction of an experimental full-scale Convoy Fighter stripped of armament, electronic equipment, etc. This experimental airplane was powered by the existing Allison 5,525 equivalent shaft horsepower T-40 turboprop engine with single speed reduction gear, modified to operate through 90°. The proposed Convoy Fighter was powered by the advanced XT-40-A-B turboprop engine having 7,500 equivalent shaft horsepower and two-speed propeller reduction gear.

This experimental Convoy Fighter had the advantage of being the same structurally and aerodynamically (except for power) as the tactical airplane and could be converted at a later date to a full tactical airplane by replacement of power plant and installation of military equipment. It was pressurized, allowing for testing at high altitude, thus simulating actual operation of the tactical airplane.

The overall program for development of the Convoy Fighter could be materially shortened by designing and manufacturing this stripped down version of the Convoy Fighter rather than designing and manufacturing two different airplanes.

Preliminary Hovering Tests

A study was made of the practicability of conducting preliminary hovering flight tests with the airplane restrained. This type of testing allowed the pilot to become familiar with hovering control prior to actual takeoff. The restraining cables were controlled by three operators, one for restraint in the vertical sense, one for pitch and one for roll. This test could be conducted in any hangar with a minimum opening of 50 x 50 ft with an overhead truss strong enough to with-

31-32) SAC charts summarizing the key physical and performance characteristics of Convair's 0.766 scale prototype of the Convoy Fighter.

33) Cover to Convair's proposal for a stripped down full-scale Convoy Fighter dated 1 November 1950.

▲ 34

stand a 12,000 lb applied load based on suitable factors of safety. This test was based on the assumption that suitable support of the airplane could be obtained at the end of the fixed propeller shaft.

Correspondence & Cost Proposal

In a letter accompanying the proposal documents dated 14 November 1950, Convair noted that emphasis was placed on experimental shop methods in order to expedite construction of the prototype Convoy Fighter. It was felt that the shortest elapsed time for manufacturing was of prime importance, in order to give maximum time for test flying and early construction of the tactical airplane.

In the design of Convoy Fighter, emphasis was placed on design for high production, thus facilitating the use of feeder shop methods for subassemblies. Special attention was given to the mating problems of major assemblies.

Extensive study was given to ease of service and maintenance particularly as the Convoy Fighter had inherent advantages as a Marine Corps support airplane wherein it would be operated from advanced areas. Outstanding features of the proposed designs were:

1. Satisfactory stability and control in vertical flight and in the transition to horizontal flight based on powered wind tunnel tests of the proposed design conducted by Convair.
2. Complete freedom from buffet at all angles of attack based on wind tunnel tests and on flight tests of the XF-92A (7002) delta wing airplane of similar

34) **This artist's impression of the Stripped Down Convoy Fighter is the same one used for the production version shown on the cover of this book.**

35) **Performance and weight summary for Convair's Stripped Down Convoy Fighter.**

36) **Illustration showing Convair's proposal for tethering the Convoy Fighter during preliminary hovering flight tests; a similar setup was actually used during testing of the XFY-1 Pogo at Moffett Field in April 1954.**

PERFORMANCE SUMMARY

PERFORMANCE DATA *

TAKE-OFF GROSS WEIGHT	LB	13,830
FUEL	LB	3,480
BASIC FLIGHT DESIGN GROSS WEIGHT (TAKE-OFF GROSS WEIGHT MINUS 40% FUEL)	LB	12,440
HIGH SPEED, BASIC FLIGHT DESIGN GROSS WEIGHT		
@ 35000 FT ALTITUDE	KNOTS	504
@ SEA LEVEL	KNOTS	472
RATE OF CLIMB AT SEA LEVEL		
@ TAKE-OFF GROSS WEIGHT	FT/MIN	10,000
@ BASIC FLIGHT DESIGN GROSS WEIGHT		11,300
TAKE-OFF TIME (STANDSTILL TO FLYING SPEED)	SEC	24.8
TIME TO CLIMB TO 35000 FT ALTITUDE (FROM STANDING START)	MIN	6.4
RATE OF CLIMB AT 35000 FT ALTITUDE BASIC FLIGHT DESIGN GROSS WEIGHT	FT/MIN	3500
SERVICE CEILING AT BASIC FLIGHT DESIGN GROSS WEIGHT (100 FT/MIN RC)	FT	44,000
ENDURANCE AT SEA LEVEL		
(A) AT REDUCED POWER (362 KNOTS AIRSPEED)	MIN	83
(B) AT TAKE-OFF POWER (472 KNOTS AIRSPEED)	MIN	48
(C) AT REDUCED POWER AFTER FUEL ALLOWED FOR 10 MIN. WARM-UP, TAKE-OFF AND LANDING AT TAKE-OFF POWER (462 KNOTS AIRSPEED)	MIN	45

* ALL PERFORMANCE AT MILITARY POWER UNLESS OTHERWISE NOTED

AIRCRAFT DIMENSIONAL DATA

WING		
TOTAL AREA	SQ.FT.	346
SPAN	FT, IN.	25'8"
ROOT CHORD	FT, IN.	22'8"
MEAN AERODYNAMIC CHORD	FT, IN.	15'7"
AIRFOIL SECTION	NACA	63-009 (MOD.)
WING INCIDENCE AT ROOT	DEG.	0
AERODYNAMIC WASHOUT	DEG.	0
DIHEDRAL	DEG.	0
SWEEPBACK (LEADING EDGE)	DEG.	55
ASPECT RATIO		1.9
TAPER RATIO		5.23
VERTICAL FIN		
TOTAL AREA	SQ.FT.	150.6
SPAN	FT, IN.	19'4"
AIRFOIL SECTION	NACA	63-006.5,-009 (MOD.)
SWEEPBACK (LEADING EDGE)	DEG.	40
ASPECT RATIO		2.47
TAPER RATIO		3.15
FUSELAGE		
LENGTH	FT, IN.	29'5"
WIDTH (MAXIMUM)	FT, IN.	5'0"
DEPTH (MAXIMUM)	FT, IN.	8'10"

POWER PLANT

UNIT	ALLISON 5525 ESHP T-40 TURBO-PROP ENGINE
SPEC.	BASED ON ALLISON DIVISION OF GENERAL MOTORS CORPORATION SPEC #300 DATED 1 MARCH 1950
PROPELLER	8 BLADE DUAL ROTATING - 15.5' DIA., AF = 150
	DESIGN $C_L = 0.35$
	GEAR RATIO = 13.65:1

ENGINE STATIC SEA LEVEL RATINGS

CONDITION	RPM	PROP SHP	JET THRUST (LB)	FUEL CONSUMPTION (#/HR)
TAKE-OFF	14300	5035	1225	3520
MILITARY	14300	5035	1225	3520
NORMAL (100%)	14000	4470	1115	3240

WEIGHT SUMMARY

WEIGHT EMPTY — 9,960 LB

WING GROUP	1,574
TAIL GROUP	426
FUSELAGE	835
ALIGHTING GEAR	300
ENGINE	2,585
ENGINE ACCESSORIES	290
POWER PLANT CONTROLS	30
PROPELLER	2,105
STARTING SYSTEM	30
LUBRICATING SYSTEM	100
FUEL SYSTEM	205
INSTRUMENTS	50
SURFACE CONTROLS	480
HYDRAULIC SYSTEM	260
ELECTRICAL SYSTEM	251
COMMUNICATING	139
FURNISHINGS	245
AUXILIARY GEAR	55

USEFUL LOAD — 3,870 LB

PILOT	200
FUEL	3,480
OIL	80
TRAPPED FUEL AND OIL	75
EQUIPMENT	35
GROSS WEIGHT	13,830 LB

CONVAIR
ALTERNATE

▲ 35 ▼ 36

configuration.
3. Inherent structural rigidity of the delta wing planform resulting in suitable wing tip installations of armament complete outside the propeller plane.
4. Compactness of design which was ideal for shipboard operation.
5. High ground stability (against overturn) through installation of alighting gear at the vertical surface tips and at the wing tips resulting in maximum operational flexibility.

Convair emphasized its proposal for a stripped down version of the Convoy Fighter powered by the existing 5,525 equivalent shaft horsepower Allison T-40 engine with single speed reduction gear and modified as required to operate through 90°. This airplane had the advantage of being the same structurally and aerodynamically (except for power) as the tactical airplane and could therefore have been converted to a tactical airplane by replacement of the power plant and installation of military equipment. Immediate design and construction of this full-scale stripped down Convoy Fighter, in lieu of a 0.766 scale prototype, effectively reduced overall cost and elapsed time of the entire Convoy Fighter program.

As required by BuAer, Convair guaranteed the following:
1. Weight empty within 2%.
2. Takeoff gross weight as shown in the proposal, with the provision that the weight may vary, within the limiting requirement of a 5 ft/sec² minimum acceleration during transition from vertical takeoff to normal climbing flight.
3. Performance as shown in the proposal, without tolerance.

The cost proposal followed on 29 November 1950. In its letter to BuAer, Convair noted that the Navy had requested that the Convoy Fighter proposal be prepared in two parts, Part One covering two scale prototype airplanes and flight test thereof and Part Two covering two full size experimental Convoy Fighters, one static test article and flight testing. It was understood that Part Two would be initiated only after the flight tests of the scale prototype indicated soundness of design. Convair prepared its proposal on these bases and in addition presented a Part Three as an alternate to Parts One and Two. The proposed Part Three contemplated the construction of two airplanes and a static test article. The first of the two airplanes would be a stripped down version of the tactical article utilizing the existing Allison T-40 power plant. The airplane would be structurally and aerodynamically the same as the tactical article and would be converted later to the full tactical airplane by the addition of military equipment and replacement of the power plant. It was believed the alternate Part Three program complied with the intent of the invitation and offered definite advantages from overall cost and schedule considerations.

The estimated cost for Part One was $2,643,511.60 and for Part Two was $4,265,792.60, or a total of $6,909,304.20. The estimated cost for the alternate or Part Three was $4,756,741.40. Assuming authorization to proceed was received during January 1951, the following first flight dates were established:
- Part One Scale Prototype: First Airplane – May 1952, Second Airplane – July 1952.
- Part Two Experimental Convoy Fighter: First Airplane – April 1954, Second Airplane – August 1954
- Part Three (Alternate): First Airplane – August 1952, Second Airplane – December 1952

Based upon the estimated costs, Convair was prepared at any time to negotiate a fixed price or cost plus fixed fee contract. For this purpose Convair anticipated a 10% profit factor for a fixed price contract or a 6% fee factor for a cost plus fixed fee contract.

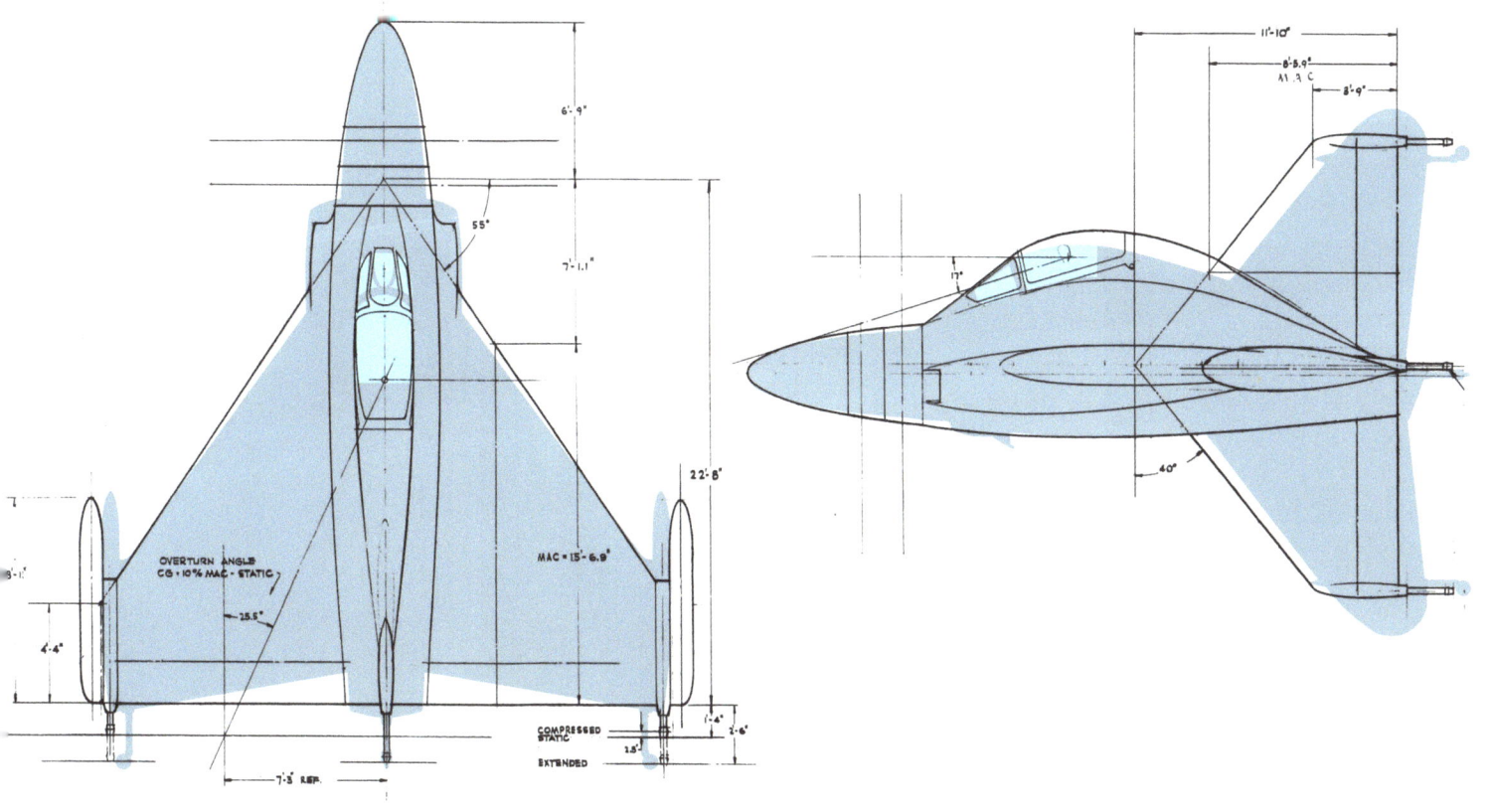

▲ 37

Success and Failure

As discussed in the previous Convoy Fighter monographs, overall gross weight was likely a key factor in determining the winners of the OS-122 competition. Convair claimed that their takeoff gross weight was 16,000 lbs, meeting the requirement. BuAer's calculation put the weight at 16,724 lbs, notably above Convair's estimate. Despite this, by BuAer's calculations Convair's proposal was the lightest of those submitted, with Lockheed coming in second at 16,813 lbs. It is no accident that both companies were awarded contracts in May 1951 to build and test their respective versions of the Convoy Fighter.

Convair's selection of a delta wing con-figuration may have aided its victory, giving it an edge in weight and maneuverability over its rivals. The company's experience with the delta wing XF-92A gave it added credibility. Lockheed's more conventional straight wing submission may have been chosen as a back-up in case the delta wing type failed to meet expectations.

Following the advice of Convair, BuAer elected not to build the 0.766 scale prototype, focusing instead on the stripped version of the full scale aircraft. Three XFY-1's were built, with the first being used for engine testing; the second used in actual flight tests (serial no. 138649); and the third for static testing. It was powered by the Allison YT-40-A-14 turboprop providing 7,100 shp; production aircraft would have used the more powerful Allison T-54, but neither the aircraft nor the engine were built in quantity.

The first tethered flight of the Pogo was made on 19 April 1954 by Lieutenant Colonel James F. "Skeets" Coleman inside a naval airship hangar at Moffett Field in Mountain View, California. The tether set-up was similar to the illustration shown in the original proposal on p.

37) Original plan of the Convair Class VF Convoy Fighter overlaid with a silhouette of the XFY-1 Pogo as built. While the XFY-1 retained the basic configuration of the original proposal, nearly every contour was subtly altered in the type's journey from the drawing board to an actual functioning aircraft.

27. Over the course of several weeks, Coleman flew the tethered aircraft nearly 60 hours, with the first outdoor flight occurring on 1 August 1954. On the second test flight that day, Coleman flew the XFY-1 150 ft into the air. This was followed by 70 takeoff–landing drills at the Naval Auxiliary Air Station in Brown Field, California. Coleman made the first transition from vertical to horizontal flight on 5 November 1954.

Further testing revealed the aircraft's inability to decelerate and stop efficiently after flying at high speeds due to its light weight and lack of air brakes. Landing could only be accomplished by the most experienced of pilots, as it required the pilot to look back over his shoulder to keep the vehicle stable. Even with the Allison T-54, the Pogo's top speed would have been under Mach 1, putting it at a disadvantage against jet fighters capable of twice that speed. These issues ultimately led to the type's cancellation on 1 August 1955.

One could argue that the VTOL tailsitter Convoy Fighter concept was flawed from the beginning and should not have been built at all. A fully automated system was required to safely land the aircraft and early 1950s technology was not up to the task of providing one. BuAer also did not correctly anticipate the challenging development of turboprop and gearbox technology, which were rapidly overtaken by the jet engine. Finally, the lack of spoilers or air brakes to slow the vehicle down during flight transition was an embarrassing oversight.

Perhaps these problems are only evident with the benefit of hindsight. In any case, many would agree that the Navy erred in not taking a more gradual approach to the problem. If it had only built the smaller 0.766 scale prototype, perhaps in partnership with NACA or the other services (who were also interested in VTOL), it could have gathered useful data and discovered the flaws of the tailsitter concept at much less cost to the taxpayer.

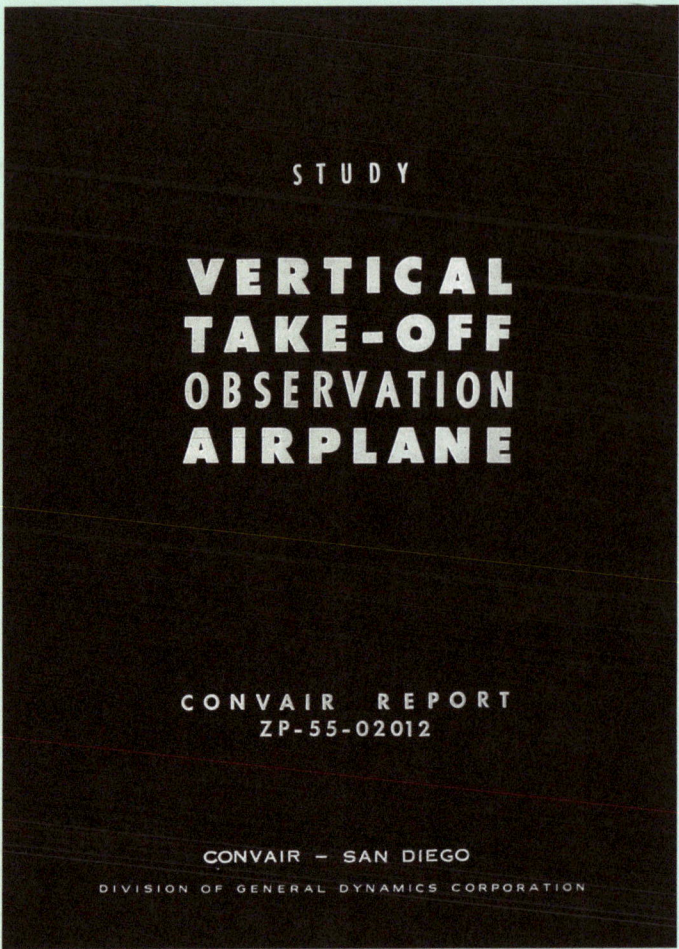

▲ 38

38) Cover to Convair's Vertical Take-Off (VTO) Observation Airplane proposal to the US Army dated 28 April 1955. This document presented two tailsitter configurations derived from the company's experience with the XFY-1.

Army Vertical Takeoff Observation Airplane Proposal

Though not directly related to the XFY-1, Convair pitched a similar tailsitter concept to the Army in April 1955 for the observation mission which is included here as bonus content for the secret projects enthusiast. According to the proposal document, during the previous 4½ years Convair had been engaged in intensive research and engineering development of various types of aircraft designed to take off and land vertically. These studies were based on the philosophy that vertical takeoff aircraft should not require special takeoff or landing facilities; i.e., they should be capable of landing practically anywhere. The feasibility of the vertical takeoff aircraft was demonstrated by extensive wind tunnel tests, by flight tests of remotely controlled models and many actual flights of the Navy XFY-1 Pogo. Transition from vertical to horizontal flight had been demonstrated for both the takeoff and return to complete the actual vertical descent to a landing.

The following is Convair's engineering review of the application of a vertical takeoff airplane design to a two-place high performance Observation

▲ 39 ▼ 40

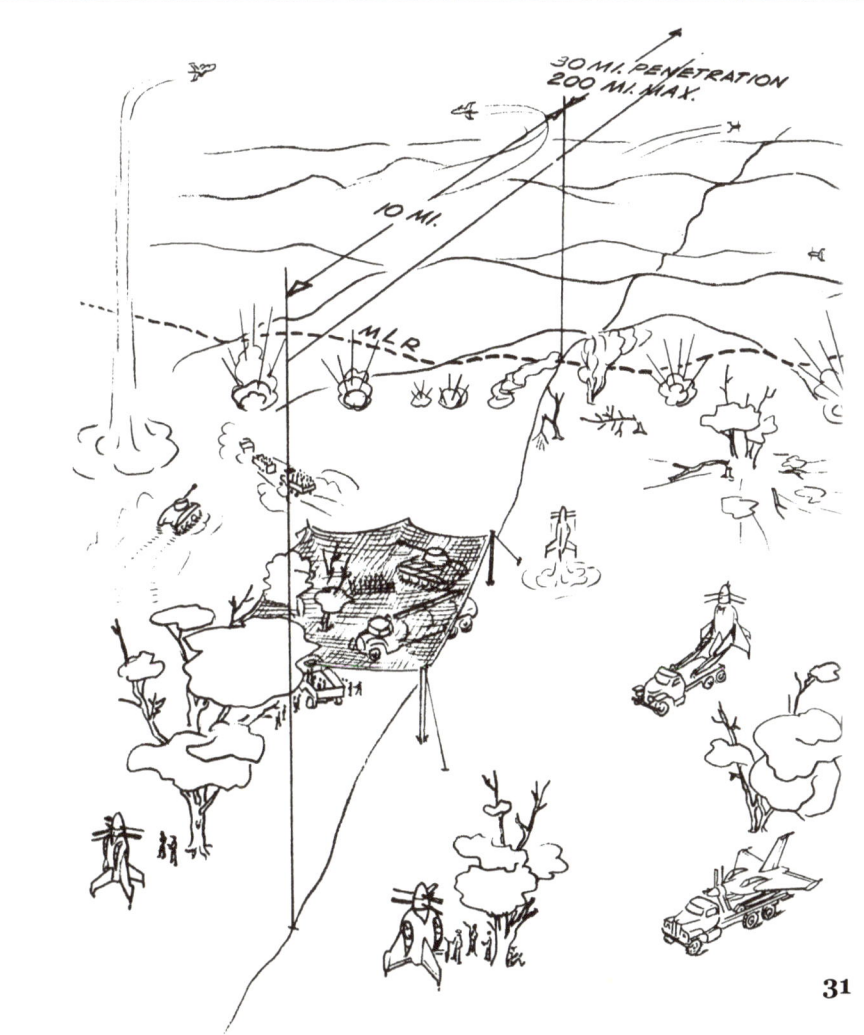

39) Artist's impression of the Convair VTO Observation Airplane study of 1955. The unusual double bubble canopies are noteworthy.

40) Concept of Operations illustration showing the potential versatility of Convair's VTO design.

TABULATED PHYSICAL CHARACTERISTICS

	WING	VERTICAL
S	150 ft^2	60 ft^2
b	18'-0"	8'-0"
AR	2.17	1.07
TR	7.64:1	2:1
C_R	14'-7-1/2"	5'-0"
C_T	1'-11"	2'-6"
MAC	9'-10"	3'-11"
Λ @ L.E.	55°	30°
NACA Section	63-009 (mod)	63-009 (mod)

Engine: Allison T-56 (501-D7) Turbo-prop (alt. T-38)

Propeller: (for T-56) 13'-6" dia. 6 blade dual rotation
R.P.M. = 977   Activity factor = 140
Design lift coefficient = 0.5

ESTIMATED WEIGHT

Wing group	542 lb	Fuel system	51 lb
Tail group	200	Instruments	47
Fuselage	361	Surface Controls	146
Landing Gear	237	Hydraulic System	150
Nacelle	86	Electrical	159
Engine Installation	1610	Communicating	62
Engine Accessories	152	Furnishings	323
Power Plant Controls	19	Weight Empty	5340
Propellers	1090	Useful Load	1273
Starting System	25	(incl. 800 lb fuel)	
Lubricating System	80	T.O. Gross Weight	6613 lb

▲ 41

and Reconnaissance airplane capable of:
1. Operating from forward area bases.
2. Landing and taking off vertically from small, cleared areas.
3. High rate of climb and acceleration.
4. High speed cruise to and from target area.
5. Slow speed of less than 50 knots (kts) for reconnaissance.
6. Loiter time over target of three hours or more.

VTO Observation Mission

For the purpose of establishing design criteria, it was assumed that this VTO airplane would be employed with artillery batteries and field forces as described below and would have certain general characteristics also described herein.

Convair assumed that it was desirable to operate the aircraft in small groups of two to four airplanes directly from various field command posts at approximately ten miles behind the MLR (main line of resistance). The airplane had to be capable of takeoff from a concealed, unprepared area and had to be able to penetrate up to 200 miles from enemy territory. However, an average penetration of 30 miles was considered to be required for a typical mission.

The airplane had to be as small as possible as an aid to ground handling and camouflage. Provisions were required for a pilot and an observer with a wide range of visibility. Provisions for tilting the pilot and observer seats forward and backward were also provided. Rotation of the observer's seat was considered for horizontal flight. The observer was replaceable with photographic equipment when desired.

General Design Considerations

In order to determine the feasibility of a small vertical takeoff airplane designed to perform the mission outlined previously, the power output per pound of weight of a number of engines in the small and medium power class was examined. The horsepower per pound with dual rotation gear box for reciprocating engines investigated was found to vary between approximately 0.52 and 0.88, which was considered insufficient for efficient VTO design. The horsepower per pound for the turboprop engines varied between approximately 1.57 and 2.22. Turbojet engines were not considered for this application because of their excessive fuel requirements.

Based on the use of a turboprop power plan, a preliminary design chart was prepared. The chart indicated a minimum attainable value for several design parameters necessary to meet takeoff conditions as follows:

Minimum takeoff weight	6,000 lbs
Minimum horsepower	1,400
Desirable propeller diameter	13 to 14 ft

A slightly higher weight and power were required if a good margin of takeoff performance was desired to permit operation on hot days or from high altitude terrain. The increased power is also required to meet the 500 kt maximum speed.

Description

The T-38 and T-56 engines were selected

41) Physical characteristics and weights of Convair's VTO Observation Aircraft study for the Army.

42) General arrangement drawing of the Convair VTO Observation Aircraft study. At 22 ft 8 in long, it was substantially smaller than the XFY-1, which was 32 ft in length.

as the only domestic power plant in the desired power range which was already in flight status. The T-56 engine offered greater power and superior specific fuel consumption with negligible penalty in overall installed weight. Design studies were made based on the use of the T-38 or T-56 interchangeability.

The delta wing planform was selected because of its aerodynamic superiority in the transition range at high angles of attack. Wind tunnel and flight tests had shown it was possible to slow to zero velocity with this configuration smoothly without changing altitude. The use of suitable airfoil camber and wing twist permitted good cruising performance to be obtained. Since the airplane mission did not require Mach numbers in excess of 0.9, no high speed design problems would occur with this type of airplane configuration.

The upper and lower vertical tail arrangement ensured a stable ground platform and provided adequate aerodynamic directional stability for all phases of flight. The ground attitude of the airplane was tilted forward slightly by the shock strut arrangement of the vertical tails. This was done so that the ground attitude coincided with the estimated hovering trim attitude.

The forward location of the pilot and observer ensured a wide range of visibility for both pilot and observer.

Provisions for up to 2,400 lbs of fuel were included for extended range and endurance although this amount of fuel may seldom have been required for normal operation.

Robert E. Bradley's excellent *Convair Advanced Designs II* shows a third configuration of this design with the pilot and observer in separate pods mounted on the wing tips; it was not included in the copy of the report I found, so it is not reproduced here.

Performance Characteristics

The performance was based on use of the T-56 engine with ESHP rating of 3,750 and propellers at 977 RPM.

Takeoff. The static thrust at sea level under standard atmospheric conditions was estimated conservatively to be 10,250 lbs. This gave sufficient excess thrust at any loading condition to allow takeoff up to altitudes of 10,000 ft or takeoff under hot day conditions. Time from standstill to level flight at best climb velocity was approximately 30 seconds.

Landing. The time required to decelerate from a level flight approach speed of 120 kts to vertical flight at zero speed at 200 ft altitude was approximately 20 seconds and a let down from 200 ft required approximately 20 additional seconds. Flight tests had demonstrated the ability of similar VTO configurations to make satisfactory spot landings, even in cross winds.

Climb and Velocity. The aircraft had an estimated performance of 500 kts at sea level with a slightly higher maximum velocity available at altitude.

Cruise. An average mission which was initiated in friendly territory from ten miles behind the MLR and penetrated thirty miles beyond the MLR with fuel reserve for three minutes at maximum velocity at sea level and standard reserves for landing was assumed. The ferry range of the airplane was estimated to be 1,000 miles. If desired, this could have been substantially increased with additional fuel and assisted takeoff.

Acceleration Characteristics. An observation airplane of this type had to depend on its small size, speed and maneuverability for defense. In order to effectively use the speed potentialities, the airplane required very good acceleration characteristics. Preliminary calculations indicated that the airplane studied here was capable of accelerating from cruise at 250 kts at sea level to a maximum velocity of 500 kts in less than one minute.

Rejection

The Army passed on Convair's VTO Observation Airplane study and the type was never built. It should be noted that the proposal was submitted in late April 1955, about 3 months before the XFY-1 was canceled. The Army likely inquired with the Navy and found out about the problems encountered with the Pogo in flight testing, concluding that Convair's tailsitter observation airplane would have similar flaws, making it a less useful and reliable platform than the company claimed.

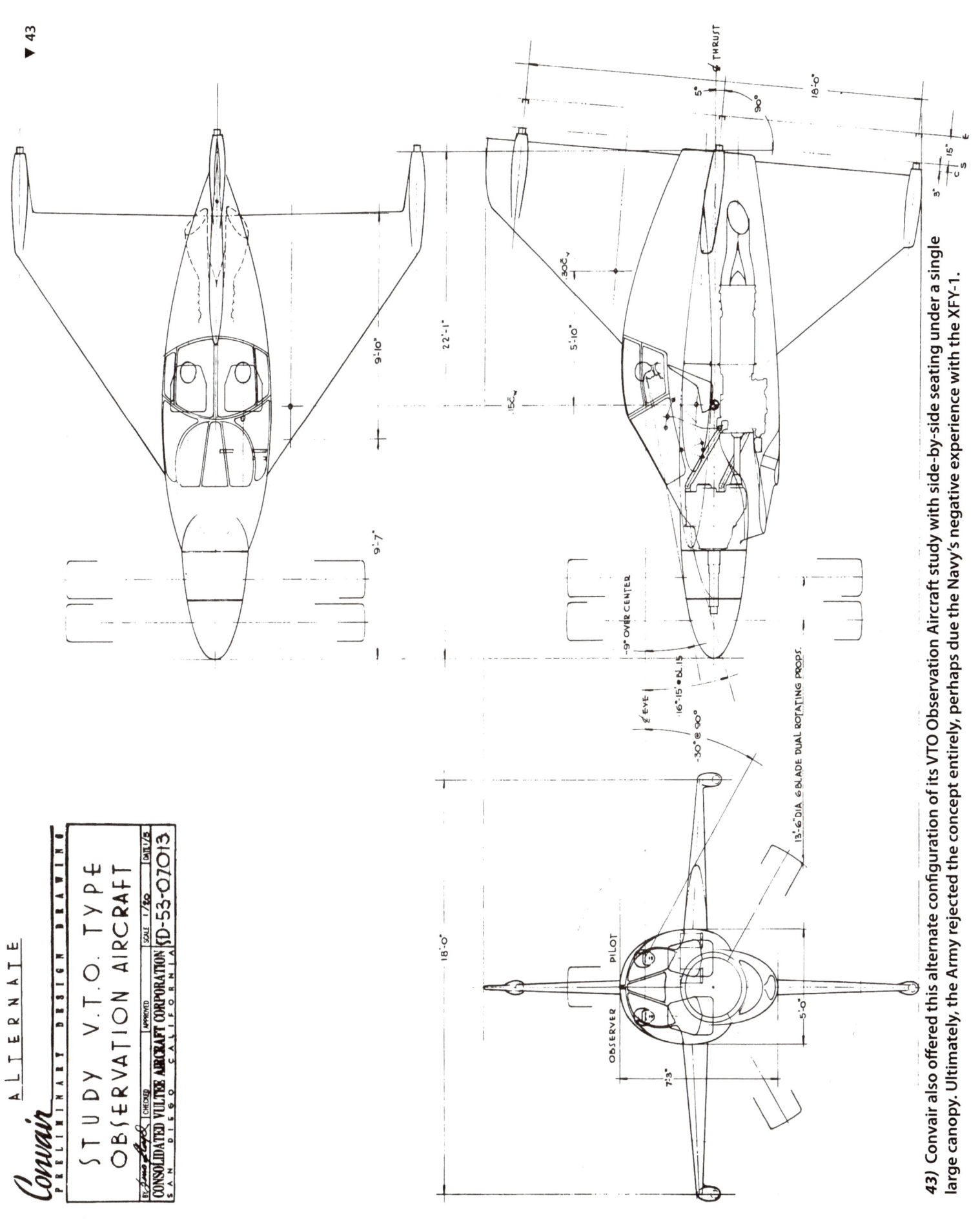

43) Convair also offered this alternate configuration of its VTO Observation Aircraft study with side-by-side seating under a single large canopy. Ultimately, the Army rejected the concept entirely, perhaps due the Navy's negative experience with the XFY-1.

Gamby Vertigo Plane of 1933

The VTOL tailsitter aircraft concept did not emerge in 1950; the basic idea went back many years before, as illustrated by the design discussed here. While only tangentially related to the Convoy Fighter concept, it is included to show an earlier take on the tailsitter idea and round out the final pages of this booklet.

On March 12, 1934, Georges Henri Gamby of Santa Monica, California submitted his Vertigo Plane concept to Chairman Joseph S. Ames of the Aeronautical Patent and Design Board at the War Department. There is scant information available on Gamby, who appears to have been an amateur inventor of French ancestry; English was definitely not his first language, judging by the spelling and grammatical errors in his letter to the government. He had some basic knowledge of aircraft construction and blueprints; perhaps he worked on the factory floor of a local manufacturer like Lockheed or Douglas.

According to his proposal, the Vertigo was designed to rise straight up and assume horizontal flight after clearing obstacles, the lift and forward propulsion being maintained by two large contra-rotating propellers mounted on the nose of the plane. The propellers were geared to a lower speed than that of the engine, a Warner 110 H.P., and revolved in opposite directions to equalize the torque. The lower propeller or "rotator" turned with an oscillation motion (not shown in the accompanying drawing); Gamby believed this movement to be essential for the aircraft to achieve *décollage* (takeoff) from the ground. The controls were the same as those of a conventional airplane, with only the pilot seat pivoting according to the position of the vehicle. The assembly and riveting were of Gamby's own design, permitting the use of rivet squeezers for almost the entire construction, eliminating the use of bucking bars.

Additional details of the design can be gleaned from the blueprint. The huge broad chord propellers/rotors had a 19 ft diameter; in contrast, the bullet-shaped fuselage was short and compact, with an overall length (or height, depending on the attitude) of only 11 ft 5 inches. The huge propeller disc would have restricted the maximum speed of the aircraft in horizontal flight. The large canopy featured ample transparencies for the pilot to view the ground during landing, though no ventral window was provided. No provisions were shown to channel cooling air to the radial engine. The wings were all-moving with no separate ailerons or flaps. The large tail was of cruciform configuration. The fixed landing gear featured prominent bracing struts, which would have created significant drag.

Rejection

The National Advisory Committee for Aeronautics (NACA) evaluated all the proposals sent to Aeronautical Patent and Design Board, which was set up by Congress to promote aeronautical innovation through monetary awards. G.W. Lewis, Director of Aeronautical Research, found little merit in Gamby's design. In his letter dated March 28, 1934, Lewis noted that identical arrangements had been proposed and Gamby's airplane was neither newer or better than its predecessors. The Vertigo provided no means whereby control of the altitude, attitude, and position could be effected below flying speed. As an airplane, the arrangement would be unstable and uncontrollable; hence, it was unable to accomplish the purpose for which it was intended. No award was recommended.

Likely discouraged by this response, Gamby never formally patented his design or attempted to build a prototype, as far as the historical record shows.

▼ 44

44) Original title block to the Gamby Vertigo Plane blueprint. The general arrangement has been traced to improve clarity and is shown on the opposite page. NACA considered the Vertigo completely unworkable but it would make a fun modeling subject.

1/48 Scale
©2017 Jared A. Zichek

GAMBY VERTIGO PLANE MODEL-A
July 22, 1933

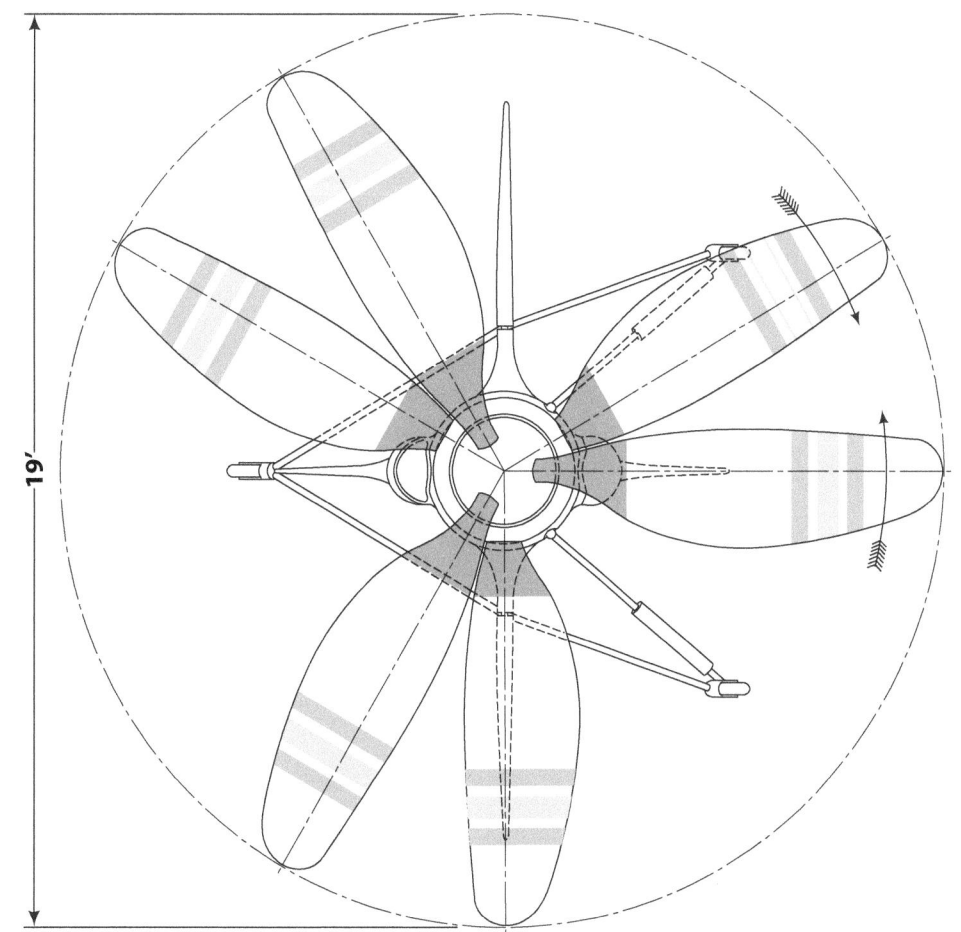
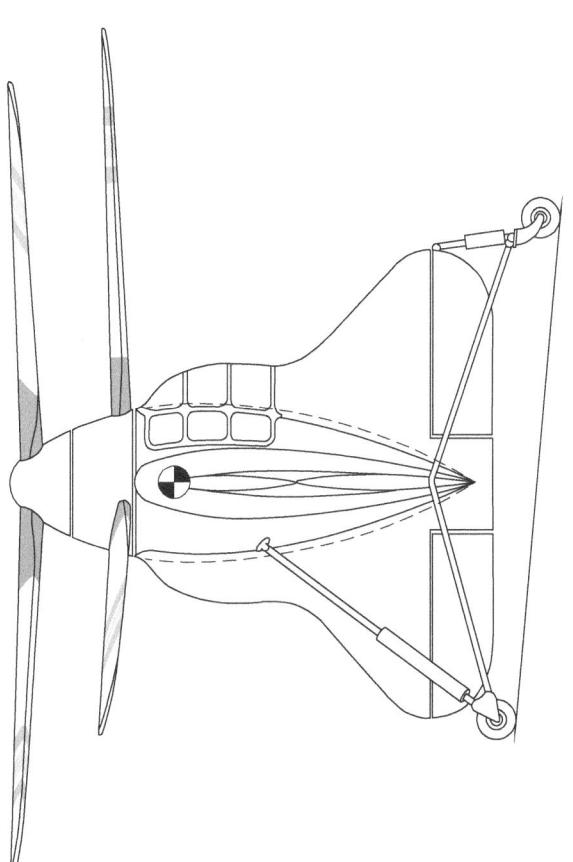
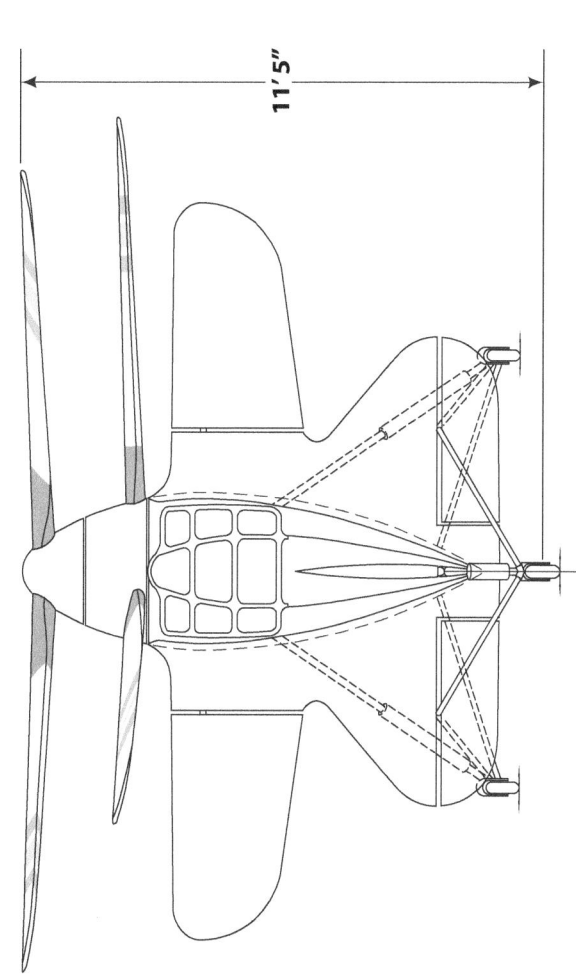